Footprint of a Heart

18,000 MILES OF STILLNESS THAT MOVES

By Shayla "Kiddo" Paradeis

Footprint of a Heart

Published by
Great Grey Endeavors, LLC
Carbondale, Colorado

ISBN: 979-8-9883928-0-4

Illustrations by Sasanka Wilson

Author photo by Beth White Photography

Maps drawn by: Christopher Crecelius
Maps throughout this book were created using ArcGIS® software by Esri. ArcGIS®
and ArcMap™ are the intellectual property of Esri and are used herein under license.
Copyright © Esri. All rights reserved. www.esri.com.
New Zealand Map: Contains data sourced from
the LINZ Data Service licensed for reuse under CC BY 4.0
United States Maps: Contain data sourced from
the Bureau of Land Management

Light of the Moon, Inc.
Partnering with independent authors since 2009
Book Design/Production/Consulting
Carbondale, Colorado • www.lightofthemooninc.com

To the sweet lady on the train who said,
"If you write a book, I'll read it."
And to the guy in New Zealand who
called me a vegetable loving luddite.

Contents

Preface

Words from a Trail Brother

She walked up to the road, stuck her thumb up with a smile, and vanished into the passenger seat of an 18-wheeler within minutes. Her tan and blue patterned hiking dress rippled as she hauled all 5'3" of herself and her pack, filled with everything she'd survived on for the past four months, into the big rig.

"I can't believe she just hitchhikes like that," my friend, Leo, said.

"Alone. As a woman!" his wife, Lindsey, added.

"Trust me, she'll be alright." I watched the northbound vehicle disappear.

We were in North Conway, NH—a small town to which this fiercely independent, hitchhiking woman, trail named Kiddo, and I had hiked 1,800 miles to reach. By this point on our trek from Georgia to Maine on the Appalachian Trail, Kiddo and I had hiked 800 of the previous miles, more or less together. I learned quickly that I could trust Kiddo based on her experience alone, which dwarfed my own. It was her fifth thru-hike in 10 years, and my first.

I was mostly used to the way Kiddo operated. She didn't have a smartphone, nor did she text or use social media. She relied on the old way of navigating the AT, a guidebook, as opposed to an interactive smartphone app that allowed even a logistical troglodyte like me to survive. She was only reachable through phone calls or email. It was a deliberate choice not to get swept up in the disconnection that's paradoxically related to the forever growing technological web that keeps the rest of us digitally tethered. She's like a relic that withstood the current of an entire society shifting around her, from a time when screens didn't dominate our attention. Whenever I was with Kiddo, I could trust that she was entirely present and prepared to pour her genuine heart into our conversations, without the universe buzzing in her pocket.

One of the many idioms repeated ad nauseam among thru-hikers was *Hike your own hike*. It meant to hike in a way that is most fulfilling to you individually and avoid getting caught up in the influence or expectations of others. Kiddo completely embodied that ideal.

We first met while hiking through the Shenandoahs in northern Virginia. My plan of hiking thirty miles to a ridgetop to enjoy a sunset dinner of ramen and Pop-Tarts was about to come to fruition. I was at a stream filling up with water when Kiddo and the third of our future trail family trio, Bard, materialized from the trees behind me. I walked and talked with them until we reached a road where our paths would split. Or at least I thought they would.

They had invited me to join them for dinner at the lodge restaurant, which was just off trail, but I declined, citing my plan of twilight ramen glory. When we reached this pivotal junction, a sign read on the trail in front of us: *TRAIL CLOSED FOR MAINTENANCE*, then *DETOUR* with an arrow pointing straight for the lodge. It was a sign, both literal and figurative, forcing our fates together. I dined with my new friends that night, including Kiddo's previous trail sister who had come to visit, Tide Walker.

The following week contained the most magic that I had felt on the trail. We spent days walking through the sweltering heat of the Virginia hills, sharing our hopes and dreams, triumphs and failures, fears and falters. Or sometimes we put on silly accents and acted out nonsensical scenarios to pass the time. Then at night we'd sing the sun to sleep, together.

In that first week of hiking with Kiddo and Bard, we grew an intimate bond that felt as though I'd known them for years. As though our souls recognized each other from previous lifetimes. I believe that's a testament to the way Kiddo approaches her relationships, with keen curiosity and void of judgment. I could feel her attention and care when she'd recall even the smallest details from our conversations: my siblings' names, my favorite animal, my birthday. All these little tidbits of information she'd file in her computer of a brain.

"When we reach Harper's Ferry, I'll be taking some time to be by myself." She reminded us throughout the week.

I knew that was Kiddo's plan as our friendship blossomed; that our Shenandoahn dream state might be ephemeral. She wanted time alone. Though she always communicated her intention clearly, I still felt sad, a bit slighted even, when she followed through with it. I was both amazed and heartbroken by her commitment to hiking her own hike. She left

Harper's Ferry before us, but I wasn't ready for our story together on the AT to be over.

Leaving Harper's Ferry, I kicked up my pace for four days to meet her in the dilapidated, yet charming town of Duncannon, Pennsylvania. My motivation was partly to see my friend, but more to prove a point, both to her and myself: keeping up is no problem for me.

My point was well taken, and the prospect of a continued friendship then seemed realistic. Kiddo and I hiked onward at the same clip, some days together, some apart, in an equilibrium between autonomy and unity.

Once in Massachusetts, the balance of our time together and apart tipped toward the former. This was fortunate for me because the trail was living up to its notoriously rainy reputation. I *did not* like hiking in the rain, but somehow, Kiddo... *did*. I'd need her positivity to make it through the seemingly endless stretch of thunderstorms tantrum free. Okay maybe not completely tantrum free, but Kiddo was sure to give me space for those.

The moisture persisted all the way into Vermont, and as I cursed the shin deep mud, I'd hear Kiddo's youthful giggle ahead of me as she danced up the trail. Honestly, it was annoying. But also uplifting. I've never met someone so adept at finding threads of positivity in difficult situations and using them to weave unwavering gratitude. She explained to me that she loved the east coast wetness because where she lived, in an off grid straw-bale cottage in northwest Montana, drought took a toll on her community in the form of wildfire. I realized that where I saw wet socks and misery, she saw a lifegiving resource to the landscape. Through that lens, my frustrations seemed small and temporary, and the walking got easier.

One especially stormy day, we were set to find reprieve in a Vermont BnB, where Kiddo's mother and trail family from 10 years prior visited her. I witnessed the reunion of Stephen, Tide Walker, and Kiddo, or as they called themselves, Dumbledore's Army. I was a bit nervous that I'd be excluded as the new face in the mix, but of course the reality was the opposite. They readily welcomed me, and made me feel like part of their family, which in hindsight is no surprise. The quality of relationships Kiddo fostered, and the quantity of love within them, was limitless. The stories, countless.

Though thru-hikers' paths inevitably diverge at Katahdin, trail family is for life. I feel honored to have made an Appalachian pilgrimage with such a beautiful soul as Shayla "Kiddo" Paradeis, to call her a friend, and to introduce her to you.

Like Kiddo's disposition and presence, her voice transcended time. Whether conversing or singing, each word that left her lips flowed like the poetry of her soles over soil. I've learned immensely from the way Kiddo carries herself after thousands of miles walking, and I know as she retraces her steps in the pages ahead, you will too.

-Daniel "Seeker" Mini

Part I

Exposition

"I went to the woods because I wished to live deliberately, to front only the essential facts of life, and see if I could not learn what it had to teach, and not, when I came to die, discover that I had not lived."

-Henry David Thoreau

Appalachian Trail 2011

2,181 Miles

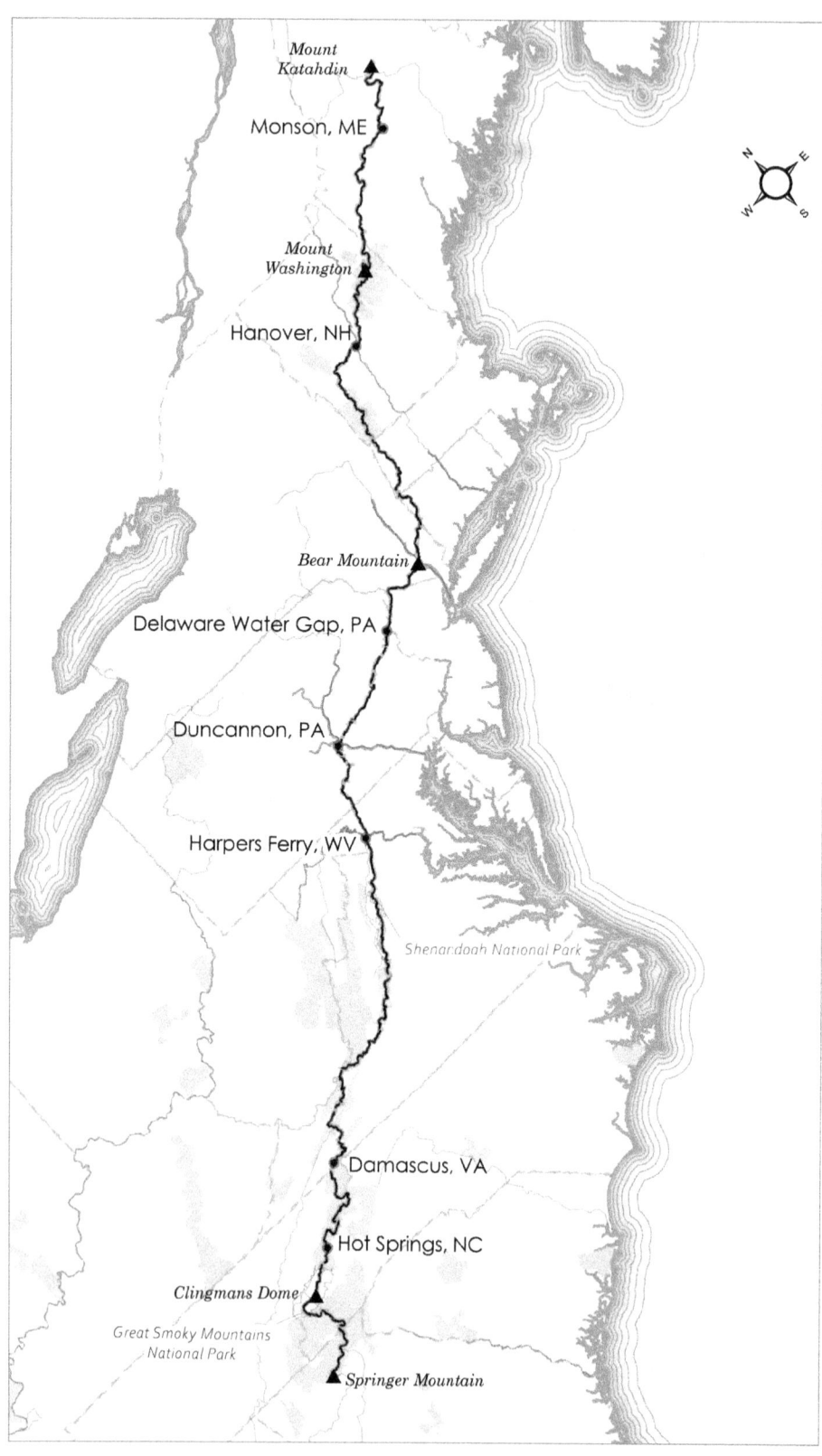

Before

February 13, 2011

With high hopes and my own two feet I walk the Appalachian Trail. From Georgia to Maine, Springer to Katahdin, the Southland to New England, and from well-fed to craving tubs of butter. This is my walkabout, where I let the land teach me how to be. 2,181 miles of well-beaten path and memories that will last forever. Lessons I hope to be brave enough to pursue.

It begins on April 1st officially. But it already started at Powell's books a few years back when I picked up Bill Bryson's *A Walk in the Woods*. Or maybe it began with my first pair of hiking boots ten years ago.

Some people might say it's crazy to walk from Georgia to Maine. Some say it's not wise, especially alone. I'm not sure that they're wrong, but I am sure that I read about the AT years ago and knew instantly that it was something I had to do. I have no idea what's in store. That's perfect.

I'm looking forward to the perspective I will gain. For understanding the distance between places and experiencing the ways they connect. For sisterhood - passing by another human being and automatically caring about them, knowing they're going through the same thing I am. For historic sites and breathtaking scenery. For dirt between my toes and hot meals tasting like life soaking back into my cells. For doing things the hard way. I expect this will only make being alive a greater thing.

This could be the best decision I've ever made.

I dubbed it "one of the best decisions I've ever made" before knowing what that decision truly was. I stuck my stick in the sand and declared my path, then promptly lost recognition that I was on one.

For each of my five long walks, I kept a blog. Each one started out centered in logistics such as gear, locations, and weather. As years and miles went by my voice evolved with my body, and words shifted toward connection, emotional health, and gratitude. I'm highlighting this first hike mostly looking back and with fewer of the original blog entries for two reasons. Firstly, the writing is not great, and I want you to like me. Secondly, it wasn't entirely honest.

When does a journey start?

In the beginning there was anticipation. With humor and a bit of pre-forgiveness, I jumped gallantly into a world where I hoped to earn my place. I figured hard work would be the key ingredient. As I had a few years prior when I attended a musical theater conservatory in Manhattan, I hit the books.

It didn't take me long to become a walking Appalachian Trail encyclopedia. I could recite the facts readily. The AT passes through 14 states. Virginia holds almost a quarter of its mileage. Most hikers go northbound from Springer Mountain, Georgia to Mt. Katahdin, Maine. A thru-hike is hiking the entirety of the trail in one calendar year. Many hikers suffer from fatigue and, scientifically speaking, starvation. Trail magic is a phenomenon of people sitting beside road crossings to support hikers with food and beverages. Trail Angels are the folks that deliver such blessings. Hitchhiking is the way to get to town to resupply. Most hikers are given a trail name which is an identity for their hiking self, implying we could be perceived as different animals than our non-hiking selves.

There were many gear decisions to make and a lot of opinions to sort through. I chose hiking boots over trail runners for footwear and opted to bring a stove to cook my food, unlike the light-weight champs who "went stoveless." Some said hammocks were where it's at, some swore by tents. I brought both for the first stretch. I also carried two books and a play to read. Numerous alumni advised me that saving weight would have been worth striving for, but this advice got lost somewhere in my German eardrums. My backpack weighed 28 pounds without food and water. Call it stubborn will, and you'd have a pretty good name for 24-year-old me.

I put together 12 resupply boxes filled with meals made of dehydrated ingredients and spices I had ordered online. I put in a candy bar for each day, then added several bags of trail mix, cereal bars, and electrolyte drink powder. I tried to guess when I would need more toilet paper or new AAA batteries for my headlamp. I imagined when I might run out of hand sanitizer and lip balm. I even made an itinerary, determining that

I'd be able to go 15 miles a day the first week, then 17 the second, and be up to 20 by the end of the third. Most hikers start with five to ten miles a day and gradually build up to an average of 15, which is a great pace for a five-to-six-month hike. I figured I could be done in four.

I wasn't capable of relaxing. My shoulders were constantly in my ears, and I walked around anticipating conflict. Coming from German-Catholics in central Minnesota and a musical theatre conservatory in Manhattan, I was ready to downregulate my nervous system. My love for being deep in the woods was wrapped in a belief that nobody could yell at me there. It didn't occur to me that I still could.

I soon learned the ins and outs of trail culture. My meals were cooked on a single burner attached to a tiny propane tank. I received the trail name Kiddo when a retired hiker accused me of looking too young to hike without an adult. I got into the rhythm of setting up my sleeping quarters every night and packing it up each morning.

For the first couple weeks I was joyful, high on fumes for an exciting new way of life. I had a supportive family, especially my two younger siblings, my mother, and my aunt, Lu. They called often and kept a map on their living room wall that showed the entire trail with a blue tack employed to represent me. Their energy was constant fuel.

I'd been accustomed to calling Lu once a week since I was a teenager. She had talked sense into me through many life hardships, like when I wanted to leave NYC while I was in conservatory. Having her support was like keeping a whiteboard of my truest emotions which I could access by dialing 10 digits. I called her crying more than once for reasons like back pain, imposter syndrome, and getting unwanted advances from men who were hiking. During one of those conversations, I told her I was struggling to "be happy all the time."

She laughed loudly. "I think that might be an unreasonable expectation, Shay. Nobody is happy all the time." Lu had a knack for knocking me out of negative head spaces.

I didn't disclose those emotions in the blog, instead I wrote stuff like this:

Time to Go Again

April 17, 2011

I spend a lot of my time on the trail thinking happy thoughts
and writing haikus. Here's a few of them:
Ode to Montana-For teaching me to layer-And to mind the bear.
Ode to Glacier Park-For making me a hiker- Strong legs and thick skin.
Ode to my homeland-For teaching me what bugs are-
This shit is nothing.
Ode to my fine feet-You little guys impress me-My apologies.
Ode to my Jesse-For knowing I'm a nutcase-And loving me still.
Ode to my fam'ly-For never ending support-And pep talk phone calls.

 *Or this.*

I Cuddled with a Squirrel

April 18, 2011

Those who know me can attest that I have a bit of an animal thing. I love
them. My cat, Max, is my best friend and I've spent hours admiring the
interactions of squirrels in Central Park, fantasizing about what great
pets they would make.

It was the squirrels that made me into a vegetarian. When I was a kid,
my dad used electric wiring in the loft of his garage to kill the supposed
pests. My ten-year-old-brain wanted none of that, and asked him, "Dad,
if I were a squirrel, would you zap me?"

His response was, "Absolutely."

Even then, I appreciated his honesty, but started feeling sorry for animals and having a hard time eating them.

I'm at the Standing Bear Farm in Tennessee, where a local man caught
on to how I love the cute and cuddly and went inside to return with his
pet squirrel. It sat on my shoulder and climbed on top of my head.

That's one more thing to cross off my bucket list.

My Appalachian Trail journey was high spirited at the start. Then came the rain. And back pain. And a jerk inside my head who reminded me constantly that I could go more miles. And told me that I should.

A walk in the woods can be anything you ask it to be. I was asking for a challenge and a chance to prove myself.

April 24th, 2011

Sitting still has been a big issue for me. I want to be moving when I'm still, but then I resent having to move too much on the trail and wish I was taking more time to enjoy spots like the one I'm at right now. I get in my head about mileage and planning and haven't yet figured out how to relax and enjoy the journey. It's got to come, in time. I hope.

Anxiety has always been a good friend of mine.

Yesterday I got to this beautiful mountain top called Big Bald. A nice family saw me hiking alone and came over to ask a bunch of questions. "Are you alone?" "Do you feel safe?" "How many miles a day?" "When did you start?" "Do you want some chocolate covered blueberries?" "Do you want an orange?" I was touched by their excitement. And I did want chocolate blueberries and an orange. I enjoyed them atop that mountain with a breathtaking, 360-degree view of tree-covered mountains as far as the eye could see. It allowed me to remember how much I love what I'm doing.

I'm still finding balance and have a little pain in my right hip, but otherwise I feel quite great. I've walked 340 miles and settled into relatively easy 20-mile days.

It feels like men outnumber women here eight to one, maybe more. It's getting to me more than it should. It's not that I don't feel comfortable around guys, I just, I don't know, miss estrogen, I guess. I'm wondering where the hell all the women are. Why didn't they want to do this like I did?

 I teamed up with two trail buddies, Stephen and Tide Walker. Stephen was internal and intellectual. Quick with an appropriate movie quote or a witty remark at opportune moments. He had southern chivalry, often reminding Tide Walker and I that, thanks to his mother's upbringing, it was his job to protect us. More often it was us looking after him, providing extra food and trying to talk him out of snap decisions.

Tide was a fierce friend. She remembered everything I told her about myself, down to my favorite nut or most ideal last meal. We bonded organically and immediately, sharing passions for things like loving the planet, movies, our cats, and independence. A fiery Aires, she could go from elated to confrontational in almost no time. Stephen and I soon came up with a warning system of whether she was High-Tide or Low-Tide.

I admired how raw she was. Envied it at times, as I felt trapped with my emotions stuffed under the surface. When she was angry, she bit, when sad, she cried, and when excited, she skipped around like a child.

We called ourselves Dumbledore's Army and carried a paperback copy of Harry Potter and the Deathly Hallows *which we had split into three pieces to share the weight. We made each other laugh and witnessed one another's suffering, getting closer than I knew how to get to most people.*

Dumbledore's Army followed my itinerary, a scribed plan of what days to get to which post offices, which I held up to myself like a stopwatch. Rushing every day, I pushed the three of us like it was my job, trimming days off our expected finish.

Half Way, Half Gallon, Half Crazy

June 12, 2011

Just another 1,090 miles to go.

After I met back up with the D.A. we passed by several historic markers in Maryland, including civil war battle sites and the original Washington Monument. We crossed the Mason Dixon line. I'm finally in the North. Then we pulled a 30-mile day on Tuesday to get us in to the halfway marker, and the ever-appealing, Half Gallon Ice Cream Challenge.

I chose mint chocolate chip. It might have been easier with a different flavor, as it seemed to feel more and more potent as I scarfed it down. While the rest of us were getting to the moaning and groaning part, Stephen tilted his carton over his head and started scraping the last bits into his mouth. For good measure, he walked into the store and got two hot dogs to eat while he watched us struggle. It was then that it occurred to me that if I was going to vomit it would be green. That made me less comfortable with continuing. But I did, and painfully finished my half gallon after 59 minutes. An average time.

That night I stayed in a mansion hostel, which was an old safe house for the underground railroad. I took a tour underneath the building to see the places where people once hid.

When I lay down that night, I felt strange, considering the things I call challenges and the way that people have treated each other.

 Guilt was driving, as though walking into the woods was walking out of my responsibilities to others. As though I owed somebody something. I had left my partner, job, and cat behind.

A fear of not belonging was whispering quietly in my ears.

In the soggy steps of the mid-Atlantic states, my spirits were quite low. Especially after a visit from my partner, Jesse, followed a week later by my two younger siblings and mother.

Once my family hugged me goodbye at a trailhead in Pennsylvania and drove off, I felt homesick. I stayed that way for weeks and didn't voice it, afraid I might quit.

Even if I did complete all the steps from Georgia to Maine, I wasn't sure if it counted as truly doing it. Some hikers considered it incomplete if you didn't carry your full-weighted pack the whole time, and I had opted to carry a lunch sack a few times in the glorious tradition of what's known as slackpacking. I wasn't sure what doing it was. Or to whom I owed that explanation.

Something in me was cracking open. I was temporarily separated from Tide and Stephen after moving at a slower pace with my mother and two younger siblings. On my own, I had opportunities to see and hear other hikers from a more compassionate place, finding myself in conversations about mental illness or losing loved ones to cancer. It planted seeds that there might be more to thru-hiking than I realized.

After meeting back up with Tide and Stephen, we came to a note on a cooler in upstate New York.

"Need a warm shower? Hungry for a home cooked meal? Call us."

I wrote in my blog post about that note that calling the number was "needless to say." But it wasn't that simple. First, I did the thing I always do, ruling out whatever didn't fit my scheduled plan. We had only walked fifteen miles that day. Tide and Stephen silently nodded and walked on, but took down the number, just in case.

An hour later, we came to a rock squeeze. It had been a maddening experience crab-walking and contorting down slippery rock surfaces, along with the way it felt entirely too designed to make my life hell while wearing a backpack. I sat at the top of a steep downhill and knew my pack would snag. I took it off and braced it in front of me, then lowered it as far as my arm would reach saying darkly, "Goodbye Neville," (I always name my backpacks) as I let it go.

It went.

It spun and bounced off jagged rocks giving me thoughts about internal bleeding. Tide and Stephen had a good laugh, which was appropriate. I chalked it up to yet another reason that what I was up to was ridiculous. Something had to give. I called the trail angel's number.

A nice fellow named Don answered and wasn't at all phased that there were three of us. Or that we would be needy in the usual hiker fashion.

He said, "I have only one condition."

"What's that?" I braced myself.

"That you shower upon arrival."

"That won't be a problem, sir." I laughed.

That night was one of the warmest nights I'd ever known. Don and Sharon picked us up and took us in like we were their nieces and nephew. They directed us to their two guest bedrooms and laundry machines and let us check our email and shower while they prepared dinner. We each gathered in their kitchen, feeling rejuvenated, and talked like family. We told hiking stories-good and ugly, exposed our fears, our struggles, and our commonality. They laughed with us about the difficulty of the New York Appalachian Trail, saying it was designed by rock climbers and known to give hikers a hard time.

I watched Stephen's hungry eyes stare at my food and felt free enough to express, "You know the way that many guys are unable to refrain from staring at your chest when you're engaged in conversation? I get the same feeling from Stephen with food. Like a dog begging."

Stephen blushed while the rest of us had a good laugh. Don patted Stephen on the shoulder and scooped up his plate to reload in the kitchen.

As the night went on, we were joined by two other hikers. I withdrew for a moment to take inventory of my surroundings. I tasted the wine. I felt the warm air from the fireplace. I heard the color and joy in the laughter around me. I appreciated the walls and the roof that kept out the rain.

*I knew that I wouldn't quit. Or at least that I didn't want to that day.
A shift in attitude walked out of their home with me, I still felt the
hardship of my body against the land, but I was able to have a satirical
sense of humor about it.*

Turkeys and Moose
and Bears, Oh My

July 11, 2011

There have been some exciting animal encounters in my recent travels.
In Connecticut, I was attacked. That's right, attacked! By a wild turkey.
So, I live to tell the tale.

I nearly stepped on a blob of feathers on the narrow path of farmland,
then jolted back as that blob got up and walked away. And there was
mama, standing tall with a certain desire to end me in every fiber of her
being. Particularly with her feet and sharp beak. She chased me like a bat
out of hell down the trail, squawking and nipping. I started running full
on, for a minute or so, and figured I would have lost her. Then I turned
around to see the angry grimace of her bobbing head back and forth up
the hill toward me. It's funny now, but at the time it was terrifying.

In another animal event near the lovely town of Dalton, Massachusetts, I was walking through sticky mud. Focused on the ground in search
of good footing, I sighed to realize there wasn't any and splashed my foot
into the shallow part of a puddle. My splash was immediately followed
by another just up the trail. I looked up from my foot. A bear on the other
side of the same puddle looked up from her paw. And we both stared like
deer in the headlights. Then we jumped back like synchronized dancers
and exerted squeals as we ran away from each other. I guess even bears
forget to look up sometimes in difficult terrain. From our new distance
we both glanced back toward each other with a sort of shrug. I told the
bear that I was sorry and wondered if she, too, was laughing at herself.

Right after crossing into Vermont, Stephen and I woke up to a very
large bull moose near our camp. Moose scare me the most of all the

creatures I encounter. This one didn't give us any trouble, but their size shocks me every time.

Last, but not least, I saw a porcupine today. Stephen and Tide see them all the time, and until today I hadn't seen one and was really wishing to. They're slow and stumbly. I could watch them waddle around all day.

My AT wildlife diary feels complete.

New England was eventful, not just for the four-legged visitors. I fell ill in Connecticut from mold in the straw of my water vessel. Under the silhouette of the mighty Berkshire mountains, I spent a night teetering between vomit fits and admiration for the starlit sky.

Sick in Salisbury

June 29, 2011

The next morning, although I had thrown up only an hour before, I thought I could walk 20 miles. It took me about 30 minutes to realize that I was being irrational and should spend the day in bed. An 81-year-old sweetheart, Maria, came to my rescue. She was listed in the guidebook for taking hikers into her home at a rate of $35 per night. For Connecticut, that's a steal. She picked me up from the nearest road right after I called her. I spent the whole day in bed and got to watch Free Willy:) It's amazing how lucky I've been on this trail. Anytime I really need something, it's been there. I have no excuse not to believe that the universe takes care of us.

The path continued to get deeper. And all the while, a quiet contemplation stirred my thoughts. What was life or the real world? Was I doing well by myself, the earth, my loved ones? Where was my heart, and how could I be so many places at once?

Passing into Vermont brought new smells and thoughts of an end approaching. I set the dial to 25 miles a day in the Green Mountains and began to experience an anxious feeling, rushing to get to the finish. In those torrents some tenderness emerged.

Lost and Found

July 12, 2011

At the Inn at Long Trail, the Irish Pub was so reminiscent I could see green grass under fog and smell sea air. And just when I thought life couldn't get better, I looked over and saw a familiar face. Cynthia, a 71-year-old woman I had helped a couple days before. She was lost, for hours, in the woods. All I did was walk with her a bit and call her husband, Ron. And since then, they'd been scoping out this restaurant in hopes to treat my friends and me to a nice dinner.

Not only was it exquisite, but they were an amazing couple to spend time with, full of life and loaded with experiences. Another hiker we knew since Virginia came along. His name is Uli. He's from Germany. And when asked why he chose the AT, he gave the best reason I have ever heard. "I have skin cancer but love the outdoors. So, when I found out there was a green tunnel I could walk in, I was immediately drawn to it." He's a tough cookie, still walking after shin splints, Lyme Disease, and Bell's Palsy since he started this hike.

 Our trio became a duo, as Stephen realized his heart wanted a different journey for the rest of his summer. After he confessed his decision to get off trail, during a muddy walk near Stranton, Vermont, I could feel the lightness in his heart.

I sat with him beside the campfire that night, deep in thought. Even though I felt envy of the relief in his eyes and the fact that it was his last night in the same shorts, I knew I wanted to continue. I knew that I could do it and was going to make sure that I did. I wanted Katahdin's magnificent view, and I could count on myself to get me there.

As I sipped my tea within the 12th state of the 14-state journey, I finally believed in myself. I was a thru-hiker, and I was going to Maine.

My heart was rekindled, but my body was another story. By the time I had crossed into New England, I had lost twenty-six pounds. My thirty-to-forty-pound backpack was now over a third of my overall bodyweight. In the White Mountains of New Hampshire, I was barely alive, waking up in cold sweat in the night and occasionally having dizzy spells and vomiting. Just when it started to look like I might not be able to move on, my mother appeared.

On top of Mount Washington, a location famous for having the worst weather in the world, she came galloping out of a railway car. The train full of people cheered as I ran into her arms.

Mama was there until the end. As a teacher, she had time off in the summer and spent it with me doing road support. She met me at road crossings and we camped together with Tide Walker, sometimes sharing cabins with other hikers who had road support.

I wish I could write something different here, but my attitude toward the trail didn't improve after she came. While my mother was an ally, the trail remained something to defeat. I walked with a light pack for the final *three hundred miles and had a skip in my step for anticipation of meeting my mother each night. But as for the surroundings, I didn't notice.*

I looked to my watch more than the mountains and listened to my busy mind instead of the forest. At a road crossing in Maine, I told my mother that I would be okay with skipping the six days I had left and bee-lining to Mt. Katahdin to get my photo and call it a game.

The hurt in my mother's eyes helped me realize what I had just said, I called it a game. I didn't skip. I walked the rest of it, then stood at the northern terminus.

Ladies and Gentlemen, It's Over

August 6, 2011

On the morning of August 6th, at 8:45 am, I made it to the top of Katahdin. It was a gorgeous day, probably the best it gets up there. I felt like I was in the sky, and the air around me was a brilliant blue. I got a little scared by the sketchy rock climbing I had to do, mostly because I knew coming down was going to be dangerous (not to mention that I'm a big scare-d-cat when it comes to heights). Regardless, I made it up there in great spirits, sat by the infamous Katahdin sign, ate my last hiking meal, and looked south feeling peaceful and satisfied.

But that was all. I'd been thinking for months that the summit of Katahdin was going to bring out emotions in me I didn't know I had. I thought it was more than possible that I would cry or scream or go weak in the knees. I didn't. I thought to myself, 'Wow, this is it. Pretty.'

On my hike down, I found myself getting more and more excited with each step. I passed others on their way up and bombarded them with friendliness. The sketchy rocks weren't as scary as I thought, especially after seeing people of all shapes and sizes coming up the mountain. Including small children.

It wasn't until the very end, when I was about to get back to the campground, that I got sentimental. I stopped, looked around at the trees, and suddenly realized how much I was going to miss them. I expressed my gratitude, thanking them for the shade, the protection, and for wearing the blazes to show me the way from Georgia to Maine. That's when the beauty hit, and I knew that it was one of those moments in life that will always be with me. That no one could ever take away.

And then, it was over.

The thing about my first thru-hike is that I didn't fully experience it. I rushed to get it done. I beat myself up about being good enough or fast enough or smart enough to pull it off, and I never let up. I told myself I was selfish for not being with my partner and cat, and I treated the entire journey like a test that I wanted to ace, rather than an experience to live fully, with all five senses. I missed an incredible opportunity to be alive.

The deepest part of it came when I was back in Montana, living out what I had once called real life.

Reflections

August 23, 2011

It's been two and a half weeks since I completed the journey. I'm having a hard time putting into words how I feel. It's strange to spend time in a vehicle. To watch the miles and states roll by. It erased my hard work. Like I spent months winding up a ball of yarn, and all at once, it unraveled.

I cried the other day when I realized the sun had gone down without me noticing. Losing daylight in the woods was significant, and it certainly never went unnoticed. Sadder still, is how it all seems like a wild, fanciful dream.

The journey changed me. I'm such a feeler now. I feel closer to my loved ones, and to people I don't even know. As though every exchange has become more significant.

On the road trip back from the AT, I felt many things. Sore, for one, from my lack of butt padding (an issue I've never experienced before) and from sitting still after many months of moving forward. I was sad to be driving away from New England, and the trail itself. It felt like the end of a good relationship. As if the trail was a friend of mine that I may never see again.

When I got to Pittsburg to visit my brother, Mitch, I felt like I had never seen a big city before. I stood on the roof of his apartment, close to an impressive backdrop of shiny buildings lit up at night. I marveled, much in the same way I had in my aunt Lu's car the first time I got a good look at downtown Minneapolis. In disbelief that humans could make such things. My brother pointed out how strange that was since I once lived in Manhattan.

I went for a short morning walk and looked all around me. At the buildings, the people, the cars, and the trees. I felt in tune. Like my eyes were good and open. I noticed my heart beating in my chest and my tired feet aching slightly against the pavement. I started grinning at each person that walked by as though I held a secret. I did. I was the luckiest person alive for my beating heart and aching feet.

It's hard to accept how quickly the A.T. has melted out of my life, though not completely. I was sad when my final scabs rubbed off my shins. And though weight gain is a good thing, I'll miss my bones. I've never been so well acquainted with them. That was the body of a thru-hiker. Direct proof of the struggle and commitment and longevity and sacrifice. I lost 18% of my body.

Driving back to Montana was almost too easy. I didn't get bored or tired, I've gotten accustomed to being alone with my thoughts. Even as I write this, I feel glad to have time again to reminisce and pay respect to my journey. Like my consciousness is my best buddy, and I haven't spent much time with her lately.

I learned so much. The biggest lesson being about bravery. Which I think means having faith. It means believing that you can go on, even if you're scared out of your mind. Even when you think you've got nothing left. It's approaching the world with an open heart and wide-spread arms, not because you're fearless, and not because you're naive, but because you chose to believe that life is good. That people are good. And that you've got everything you need right there with you.

 Perhaps that was the true beginning of the journey.

Part II

Rising Action

"Life is what happens to you while you're busy making other plans."

-Allen Saunders

Pacific Crest Trail 2013

2,665 Miles

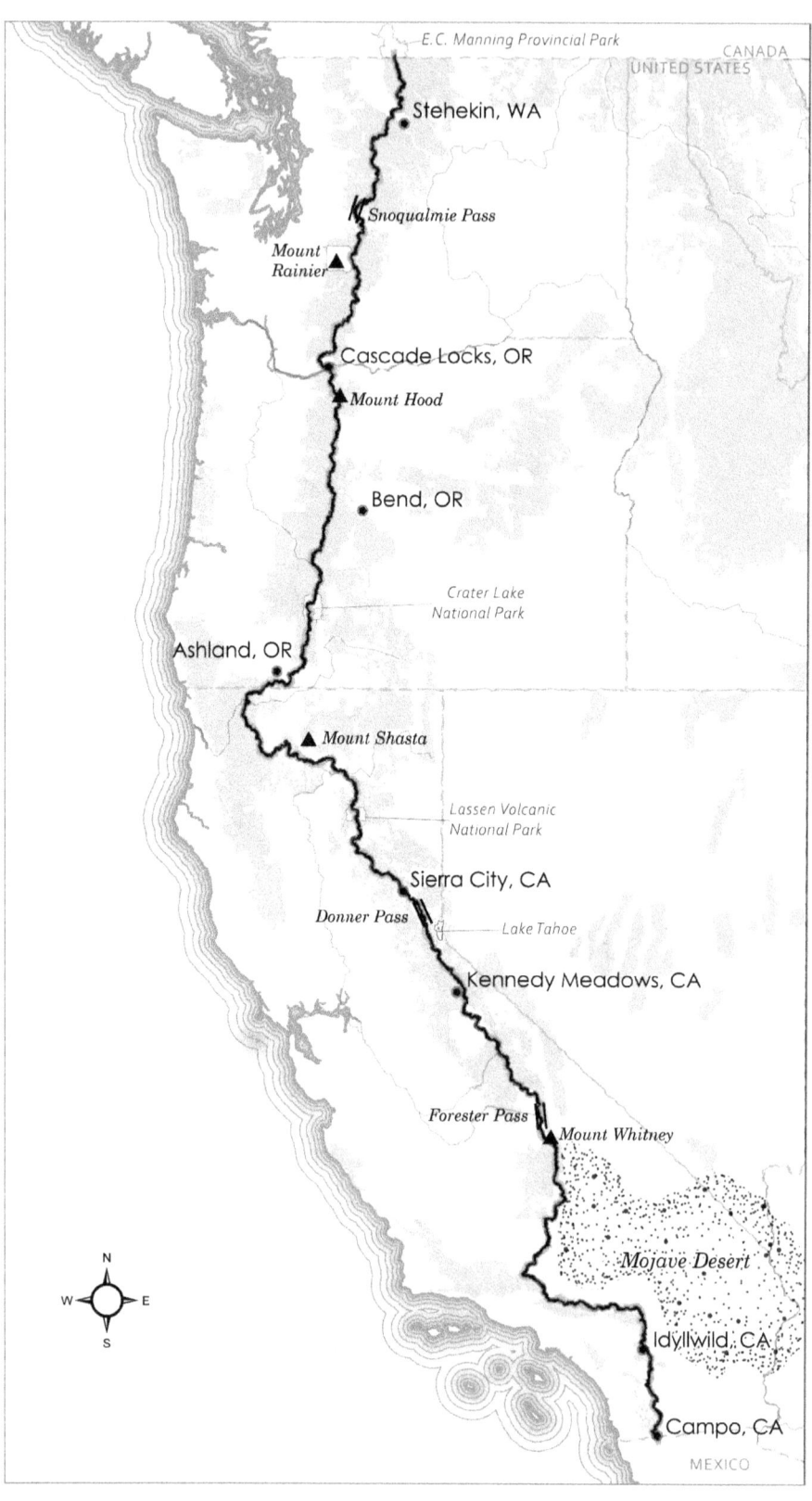

Post trail depression, PTD, is a common term among distance hikers. It is a seemingly unavoidable imbalance, likely chemical, though in my eyes it was pure heart. When life was once rainfall and pine needles, what do you make of Netflix and silicone? How do you explain yourself at the tables of friends and family? How do you relate?

Jesse and I grew distant. Seven years into our relationship I was ready to step closer. As though my wild oats had been sowed. I came home from the AT with an honest offering of deeper commitment. One which fueled us to go back to school and "get our lives together."

We rented a carriage house behind an historic site in downtown Missoula, Montana, where the wide Mount Sentinel was marked with a concrete "M". Branded like cattle. Jesse took two classes without much enthusiasm. I took five and declared a major of Health and Human Performance, thinking there was some sort of adult way to be an adventurer.

I sat surrounded by questions about statistics. I had answers, a million of them, but none of them answered me.

After 10 weeks of class, I found myself in my advisor's office trying to call upon the twinkle I'd once witnessed in his distant stare while he talked about being young and wild.

"What is the purpose of being in here?" I pointed to the open textbook on his desk. "I'm learning about land, human interaction, cultures, how we learn, what our bodies can do...but it costs more, keeps me stagnant, and is considerably less potent than being out there."

He gazed out the window where I was pointing, then at me over the rim of his reading glasses. I had told him all about thru-hiking. His lips began to curl into a tucked-in smile. "School isn't the only path."

It was the blessing I had come for. I stood up feeling better. And worse.

I had promised Jesse that I was done having big adventures without him. A month before, I'd proudly turned down a paid offer from a mapping company to hike the Pacific Crest Trail. I patted Jesse's back while I made the statement into my phone, walking beside him on the core trail next to the Clark Fork River. Jesse neither smiled nor glanced toward me.

Over the course of the following year, the life I was forcing seemed to deconstruct. My relationship with Jesse ended. My little brother was diagnosed with a psychosis that no one could explain. My health was in question, having never fully recovered from the AT. I had dizzy spells, occasional black outs, and a diagnosis of Lyme disease. Something was wrong with my heart, though many tests and a take home heart monitor could only produce the results that it was overactive.

The best way I knew how to survive anything was running into the arms of the place I loved most. In the backcountry of Glacier National Park, I stood knee-deep in a mountain stream, washing my face in the sacred runoff of Sexton Glacier. It was as baptizing as anything I had ever experienced. I had no idea what life without Jesse would be. I had no answers to what was going on with my heart. And I was terrified of what was happening to my baby brother.

But I had Glacier. In the teal waters I could begin to imagine a life of my own.

I called the mapping company to see if they were still interested in hiring a hiker to take waypoints along the Pacific Crest Trail. They answered with a resounding "yes" and the momentum picked up from there.

I moved to Steamboat Springs, Colorado, following my best friends, Shasta and Heidi, and leaned into the culture of seasonal work. An entire life could be built upon a person's love for the outdoors; a dream I dared not acknowledge as someone's significant other. It was forbidden fruit. Until it wasn't.

As soon as I made the declaration life made sense. By springtime I had a good rhythm in Steamboat Springs. I had a new boyfriend, Eric, who supported my upcoming hike.

I was ready to walk. And process.

Almost That Time

April 23, 2013

I feel like life is getting away from me. Leaving me behind and changing too fast. We don't have to worry about the essentials. We don't grow our own food, build our own shelter, find our own water sources, deal with our own waste, and with a computer in everybody's pocket, we no longer need to find our way or remember facts. I'm not saying I don't participate in it. I google things, too. I'm saying that I feel lucky to control my own worries, and I chose to worry about water and shelter this summer. That's what makes me feel alive.

On the Appalachian Trial, I realized that my brain was the original TV. That I could replay scenes, listen to music, and create without any outside help. I learned that a fallen log was the original couch and a flat rock the original dining room table.

I learned that water is amazing. It can clean you, hydrate you, cool you, soothe your muscles, cook your food, and do your laundry. It's the best thing we've got.

I learned that everything makes sense when you sync to the rhythm of the sun. It can be your alarm clock in the morning, your lunch bell mid-day, and your bedtime mood-setter.

I am so incredibly grateful for my time spent learning to entertain myself.

I'm set for life. Many an otherwise painful hour of pretending to pay attention to things that don't interest me can be spent retreating into my dynamic, boundless imagination. I've lost a great portion of my ability to take things for granted. I wake up in the morning and say thank you, to my aching feet and to the sun for coming out again. Nothing is a given. Everything is a miracle. One big mess of tiny, beautiful things.

Great Expectations

April 27, 2013

Tomorrow, I head to a gathering known as hiker kickoff. I'll be camping out with trail angels, thru-hikers, and hiking enthusiasts. That should help instill some bravery and excitement. Sometimes it seems intimidating.

I chopped off 15 inches of hair today. I've wanted to donate hair for a while, and there's no better time than right before a 700-mile desert hike.

This being my last night as a non-hiker ("townie" by hiker slang) I like to lay out my expectations. Just so we can all look back later and laugh at how shortsighted I was.

1. Short hair was a good choice.
2. I will see rattlesnakes, but have my fingers crossed that I won't wake up to one cuddling under my tent.
3. The trail is going to be physically easier than the AT, but mentally more challenging.
4. The snow is going to be sketchy in the High Sierra, and my stubborn Paradeis genes might get me into a bit of trouble. But don't worry, Mom:)
5. I will have to go longer than my record eight days without a shower.
6. I will hit a physical low, where my body enters starvation mode, somewhere in the Sierras.
7. I will be super happy to reach Kennedy Meadows, the end of the desert section, but happiest to get to the Oregon border after three months in California.
8. I might go full days without seeing a single person.
9. I think my favorite section will be the High Sierras of Kings Canyon National Parks or the Northern Cascades at the very end.
10. There is going to be fantastic beer and food.
11. This will change me for the better and be breathtakingly beautiful. I will feel lucky all the time. (This prediction is kind of cheating though, because I already do.)

It's getting real. The backpack is loaded, the hair is gone, the final phone calls are going out to my loved ones, and it's time.

Here goes nothing.

Dirrrrrrt!

May 3, 2012

I've hiked 109 miles. And in the first 10 I found myself accepting that I'm going to be dirty as all get-out for the next four to five weeks. It only takes eight hours to accumulate the kind of soilage that makes a dirt river in the shower. On the AT that would have taken a good five days to achieve. The dirty trail award goes to Southern California.

I'm not struggling in the heat as much as I was afraid I would. The toughest thing is long stretches without water. My longest has been 24 miles, for which I carried five liters. There's a 30-miler coming up in a couple days. But I think I've got this.

I haven't seen any rattlers, but I might be the only one. I like to believe it's because I have a mascot who protects me. Every day I've see one small, black snake with a white stripe down its back. I call her Zippy. When she passes by, I can almost hear her say, "Way to go," in a slight but peppy voice. I asked around and no one else has seen them. Which leads me to believe she's my guardian reptile. No, I haven't gone crazy from the heat yet. I've always been this childish.

My body is holding on strong. I've been able to average 20 miles a day right out the gate. That puts me well ahead of schedule already. So far, I find it considerably easier than the AT. Way less up and down.

First Zero Day

May 7, 2013

I made it to the remarkable town of Idyllwild, the friendliest hiker town I've seen. I got together with a few other hikers two days ago and decided to hitchhike to here a day early to set ourselves up for a 30-mile slack-pack, which we did yesterday.

We managed to find a great hotel and nice locals to drive us back to the trailhead, but during the hike itself, we got rocked. Temperatures were in the mid-30s, sleet and wind were rampant, the climb was challenging, and we were playing a fun game called *keep-moving-or-die*.

I ran for it, though it still took 11 hours, and was the first of our group to make it back to the hotel room. I waited nervously until headlights flashed in the front window. The same kind man who had picked me up on the side of the road an hour before was dropping off one of my mates. His name was Matt, and he went back to the trailhead three more times that night, making sure to retrieve each member of our crew plus a few more. We thanked him profusely while he insisted on spending his entire evening helping us.

Once everyone was in, we sat in a circle on the floor passing around potato chips and ice cream while telling battle stories. There were near hypothermic moments, and the distress of having to keep moving without warm overnight gear.

After a full day of rest, we are sharing one more night. The crew consists of Rotisserie (a solo hiking woman from Minnesota), Cookie Monster (a former AT thru-hiker who carries great music), Alien (a fellow from Israel), and Rub-A-Dub (another former AT thru-hiker from D.C.) It's been great to get to know them and I hope to see them out there. We leave town on separate itineraries tomorrow.

There are hikers everywhere in this town, happy to be out of the cold rain. This morning, after I ordered a meal at a cafe, I turned to the other hikers with tears in my eyes, overwhelmed that anything should be so easy as to ask for a meal and have it arrive in front of you.

That's the magic.

Shaylasta

May 17, 2013

My favorite redhead arrived out of the blue two days ago. I made it to Interstate 15, pulled up to a shady spot, kicked off my shoes and was promptly mauled by the one and only Shasta Bacon. She just returned from a winter in Mexico and Guatemala, went home for two days, and then flew to LAX to rent a car and come find me on the trail. I have her lovely company until May 23rd.

And how do you suppose I repay her? I try to kill her on her first day hiking. She handled it extremely well, but it was a 5,000 foot climb from I-15 to here and she pulled a tough 16-mile day yesterday. She's passed out in the park right now, and we're in Wrightwood for the evening. We got in today around lunch time and were welcomed into a friendly woman's home to get cleaned up, fed, and spend the night. Tomorrow, Shasta will be my road support as she gives her blistered feet a break.

Here are some highlights of the last eight days:

Lions and Tigers and Bears-No Joke!

Deep in the lush woods near Big Bear Lake, I passed by some Hollywood stunt animals. I saw the Grizzly first, lying in a cage barely large enough for her limbs to spread. She kept lifting her head up from her arms, looking around, sniffling a little, then putting it back down. I felt like she was crying. Surely Hollywood has enough money to buy their animals decent habitat for holding times.

A lion roared, and when it did, I felt vibrations in the pit of my stomach. As I walked toward the sound, I noticed a tiger head staring above the low wall of its cage. I stared back, wondering if we were having a moment. The lines in the tiger's face reminded me of my cat, Max. I took a step closer. The tiger reared back and started snarling and growling, then leaped forward and slashed at the side of its cage. My heart skipped a beat or two. Can't say that I recall ever having been so effectively threatened in all my life. Yet I understood. I don't enjoy being gawked at either.

Baby's First Rattler

A rather large black snake was coiled up beside the trail, did its rattle thing, froze, and let me walk by without any trouble. I have to say that the nice thing about rattlers is the warning system. It doesn't seem like they want to get close to you at all. Which works for me.

The Best Oasis in the World

A couple of days ago, on an atrociously hot afternoon, I came upon a multilevel swimming paradise in the middle of the desert. With cool pools in a small canyon, hot springs in upper pools, and many happy swimmers jumping off rocks and asking repeatedly, "Is this heaven?" That very well might have been the best swim of my life...so far.

Ziggy and the Bear

The most famous trail angels I know of, Ziggy and the Bear, bought a house on the trail so they could be what they are today. I rolled in, sweaty and exhausted, then sat down with a tub of Epsom salt water in front of my feet. They have transformed their backyard into a hiker haven, with carpet and shade. I partook in their daily Burger King run (my first fast food veggie burger in ten years) and registered in their book as the 401st hiker this season.

On the way out there was a sign: "If you like what you got, PAY IT FORWARD!" Incredible.

Finally Caught That Gator

Just now, as I was walking to the library, I looked over and saw a rather familiar face.

I met Mike, or Gator in 2011 while he was finishing up his thru-hike of the Appalachian Trail. I had just found out he was going to be here a week before I started, and was hoping to catch him. There's a whole web of thru-hikers that I'm just starting to understand.

I'm settling into the trail life. When I crawl into my tent at the end of the day, I sometimes say, "Yes." Being alone doesn't feel lonely, although I often miss Eric.

With 369.5 miles down, I'm feeling frisky as ever. Thanks for all the love.

Coyote Song

May 20, 2013

Two nights ago, at the end of a 29-mile day, I came to the Angel's Crest Highway. The sun was setting, and I knew Shasta would be picking me up in moments. I crossed the road to get a better view and was compelled to sing a song called *Coyotes* by Don Edwards. It's a pretty song, and a sad one too, with a chorus that goes, "Oooooh-yip, Oooooh-yip, Oooh."

Feeling content, I went to sit by the road, got bundled up, and pulled out some Oreos, thinking life couldn't be much better. Somehow not to my surprise, a coyote crossed the road, maybe 25 feet away from where I sat. I sang the coyote song to her while she stood there, looking peacefully back at me.

I know I'm exactly where I belong.

The Not Lonely Walk

June 12, 2013

I said goodbye to Shasta right at the entrance to most hikers least favorite part of the PCT, the aqueduct walk. It's a long day of low, hot, desert walking through dirt roads beside the LA Aqueduct. My pack was heavy with six days of food and I got lost. Feeling scared with no idea how I got so turned around, I impulsively dialed my mother's number to cry about it. (Note to self: try to avoid saying the words *I'm lost* to your mother.)

I found my way soon after and called back to apologize. After a few miles, my thoughts lightened up and I was joined by a chipper hiker named Drama.

He had a nature that was a bit rebellious, though kind and easy-going. Free in a way, but subtly weighed down in another. Like a town fox, surviving well, but staring beyond the city limits after the howl of a coyote pack. A longing I understood well.

We walked on like twins for the day. Two starry-eyed dreamers, reciting poetry. It was melodic, the pitter-patter of our brains and our feet together. We spoke of many things: love the verb vs love the noun, wind turbines and the politics thereof, and how we planned to navigate the bear canister requirements coming soon. We related over life lessons learned in New York City, having both been wanderers of its corridors with a fondness for mindful stumbling. We both missed our significant others, not hiking with us.

Then, there was trail magic. Which was unexpected. A nice couple was waiting in the shade of a giant lone tree next to a barren dirt road. They had their RV and a cooler. The high of that day was 79 degrees. Turns out no suffering was required on my day across the Mohave.

I said goodbye to Drama at sunrise the next morning and began a long walk with winds that almost knocked me over many times. I made a game of it, imagining that I was an expelliarmus curse coming out of Harry Potter's wand, and the wind was a killing curse coming out of *you-know-who's*. I had no choice but to propel forward and hold my ground for the sake of all things good in the world.

I went 48 hours without seeing a soul, which I'd never experienced before. Whether it was the wind rocking my tent violently or the shades of sooty ground in a newly burned forest, I'm not sure, but I spent those two days with a sense of eeriness. Like the world might not exist. I might not exist.

I came to a highway. Cars were driving by infrequently, which eased my mind about being the last living human, but I swallowed hard as I put out my thumb. I hadn't shaken off the uneasy feeling. My box of food was in Onyx, and to retrieve it would require a hitchhike, alone. Most of my hitching endeavors had been with hiking mates.

The feeling soon passed in the passenger seat of a chatty old man who told me repeatedly how amazing I was for persevering. He gave me 50 dollars. I told him I couldn't accept it, but he wouldn't hear it. I'm relatively certain he couldn't hear it, which is why he spoke the whole way to the post office.

With his generosity, I could no longer make up excuses not to afford to stay in town, and after six days in the sandy desert I needed to get cleaned up. I got two more hitches that day, one from a nice brother and sister who grew up in the area. Another from a laid-back cowboy, who said, "You can get in, as long as you don't mind me smoking this joint." I figured that would work out in my favor. He wouldn't be able to smell me.

When I returned to the trail at Walker Pass, there were already hikers I knew sitting at the trailhead. I went from feeling alone and worried to safe and joyful. With only 50 miles left of desert, and the gateway to the High Sierra calling me, I walked on, gladly.

Surprise, Surprise

June 17, 2013

There were wings on my heels. On the day coming into Kennedy Meadows, I went the first 11 miles in four hours. Then 10 and a half in less than four. Then the heat started getting to me. I suppose it was the desert's last chance to take me down. There was a genuine, flowing, wet, cool river coming, and I hurried to get there.

I started to hear it and saw it beneath me. Everything was going to be better than okay, when suddenly I saw something else I'd been dreaming of. A man walking up the hill toward me. *That sure looks like my Eric,* I thought, *but I sure could be hallucinating.* But after I saw the sly smile spread across his face, I knew it was real. At least I hoped it wasn't a cactus in disguise, because I threw my arms around him and kissed him good (or pretty good for someone who's about to pass out).

I got into the water right away, so that I could construct sentences instead of all the "but-what the-how-where-really?" that had been coming out. He is going to hike with me for the next few days and climb Mt. Whitney. Unbelievable.

Our first night out, with a river reflecting the bright orange sunset behind us, mac and cheese, and him, I had everything. It was the true beginning of getting to know him. The backcountry has a way of stripping people down to their base.

The awkward part was that I couldn't tell him why I was set on big miles. I had a flight booked from Mammoth Lakes to surprise him at his cousin's wedding the following week. We could be a sit-com.

Hi Sierra

June 17, 2013

The mountains of the High Sierra are truly breathtaking. Even with going too fast, which is a crime. I left Lone Pine and said goodbye to Eric with a 42 pound pack and a heavy heart. I knew I had my work cut out for me. The elevation profile for the next stretch resembled shark teeth. I was planning 26-mile days through it despite the snow and river crossings, along with seven high passes, including the highest point on the PCT, Forester Pass (13,153 feet).

I hadn't seen the trail so steep before, and my legs were already tired from the big climb up Mt. Whitney (14,500 feet) with Eric, the highest mountain in the lower 48. I moved slowly and with a slight disbelief in myself.

My mood shifted when I came over the first and highest pass. On the other side was a dreamland. Bright blue alpine lakes, carved valleys, and epic ridgelines. Kings Canyon made a place in my heart with glaciated shapes and colors like my home in Montana.

It was a crime to have to run through, but even more so to run out of water treatment. I ended up having to use iodine tablets, which is yucky. I was walking by the clearest, most refreshing water I'd seen anywhere, and drinking reddish-brown water that tasted like it came from a rusted faucet in NYC. I might never treat mountain water again.

The bugs have begun their summer season. I rolled into camp hobbling and exhausted, pushing through to the last bit of daylight just enough to pitch the tent and climb in. And when I finally laid my bones down on the ground, the mosquitos jumped me. Minnesota style, where one swat takes out five. And there I was, smacking myself, exhausted and defeated, swearing and squirming like a crazy kid in the woods (which I was). Someone could probably make a living placing cameras near campsites and stream crossings, broadcasting videos of thru-hikers throwing temper tantrums.

I walked a whole day with a kind fellow called Thirsty Boots. He was rich with advice to share, not just on hiking, but life.

Every time I find myself in a risky situation, or almost in one, I think of my poor mother. She could have had a normal daughter who works at a bank. Company over snowy passes, with Thirsty Boots, was a good one to do for Mamma.

My blog posts left things unsaid. My talk with Thirsty Boots was about life, yes, but specifically the helplessness I felt for my little brother. And the pain I felt for how much stigma was around mental illness. And for mental illness in and of itself, that our culture refers to it as illness and treats it with numbing agents. I didn't know if I could talk about that with anyone. My family was desperate for things to get better. For safety. For solution. I didn't have an answer, but I was hoping for better questions.

Thirsty Boots let me process those things out loud on our traverse of the magnificent Sierras. He also held space for me to process doubt in my current relationship. Eric was sweet and supportive and yet something didn't fit. I feared my maternal instinct, how it was easier to care for Eric than myself. I recognized the risk of not working through the wounds that were suddenly so obvious in the evergreens. I wanted freedom; of spirit, of body, and of direction. I wanted to be allowed to be deep in the woods, the only place where I felt fully alive, without the idea that others needed me to be elsewhere.

Mental Health Day

June 28, 2013

The California blues may have caught me. It's been a hard rush to get here, and now I'm having a bit of anxiety about it. I keep singing Billy Joel's *Vienna Waits for You*.

Slow down you crazy child. You're so ambitious for a juvenile, but then if you're so smart, tell me why are you still so afraid?

I'm taking a zero today, not for my body. I could admit that my feet hurt, and that I pulled a furry spider off myself this morning and have alarming bug bites around my ankles. But truthfully, I'm just here because I want to try sitting still and shutting my brain off for a day.

I'm outside of Tahoe City. An amazing friend, also named Eric, whom I once worked with at Lake McDonald Lodge in Glacier has generously allowed me access to his empty apartment and keys to his car while he's out of town. A few days ago, I spent a day in his company while he showed me around the area.

It's been hard to get comfortable. Mosquitos and rain have killed my peaceful resting moments, but that's just temporary. What's really bothering me is that I feel like friends and family could use a hell of a lot more of me. So today, I'm staying by my phone. And resting.

It was then that I began to embrace myself as walking wounded. As soon as I saw myself there, I saw others, realizing that many of us were walking our broken hearts home. To touch something real with our fingertips. To heal. A hiker I had been leapfrogging opened up about his struggle with lifelong depression. A hostel owner admitted to his lonesome heart and hopes to find love. A man who was known for setting hiking records shared his grief for how much the culture was changing. And a missionary heard my fear of my maternal instinct, laughing at how it was his goal to share his life that way. He found it ironic that I was rejecting that quality in myself.

It became evident that we were all family, and I started to understand the need for connection. I began to look for friends and to expose my heart.

Bye Sierra

July 2, 2013

Sierra City. City is a strong word. I was planning a short stop but ended up staying the night. Mostly because something happened that I've been hoping would happen since Mammoth: I caught up to the bubble of hikers I know. Roger Dodger, whom I haven't seen since Kennedy Meadows (500 miles ago), and Beads, whom I last saw at Ziggy and the Bear's house (990 miles ago). Old friends, in this culture.

At lunch, Beads and I were both realizing that we had the same rush-too-much problem. We're reminding each other to chill out. I've been trying to talk myself out of towns to save money, but this one has a bar with air conditioning that you can hang out in all day, shower, do your laundry, and camp in the back yard. No charge.

As for my California blues, I'd say it's clearing. The halfway post is in sight, my mom and brother will be visiting me in a couple of weeks, and before I know it, I'll be in Oregon. The terrain is getting much easier. Now 30 miles goes by without effort.

People make the experience.

I got a meaningful bookmark from my dad and stepmom, Sue. A tribute to my aunt, Jane, who died in a military helicopter accident when I was three. Jane paved the way for a lot of women, being a military pilot in the 1980s and forcing the baseball team of her local high school, all boys, to make room for her to play. This summer she was inducted to her high school Hall of Fame.

When people ask me why I go fast on trails, I explain that I come from Germans.

Volcanoes

July 14, 2013

I am humbled by volcanoes. How easily we could be gone tomorrow. How I might get proud of myself for walking this far, then remember that a rock could end me. A bug even, or an overlooked decision. I think of how I could run as well as Carmelita Jeter (no, I couldn't) and still, a pebble could bring me down. I spend time worrying about all kinds of things, but for some reason, these volcanoes comfort me. Imagine how small my cell phone bill will seem when this baby blows.

Five days ago, I got my first look at Mt. Shasta, the gateway to the Pacific Northwest. I once lived in Seattle and love this part of the world: the forests, the coffee, the local farms, the innovation, and the beer. I appreciate the varied shades of green and the fresh smell of ocean air.

I have gratitude for life being temporary, and for it being constant.

Upon arrival to the land of volcanoes, I was greeted by the most magic I've ever seen in one day. Starting with a trail camp in the morning hosted by angels named Pocahontas and Legasaurus. They set up a resting area with heaps of food and cold sodas. Then in the town of Old Station where I ate my lunch, I was given a beer and a Gatorade, by two hikers.

In the afternoon, I stopped along a highway to get some water before hitting a dry stretch. There were two men making sandwiches in the back of their pickup. They offered me a beer, and when they found out what I was up to, they leaned in like proud uncles. We sat on their tailgate as they fed me snacks and showed photos of their grandchildren.

I walked away feeling sad to say goodbye and didn't get far. A few steps down the pavement, they called me back with their wallets out. One of them handed me a 20, the other a 50. I shook my head with tears in my eyes, refusing to reach toward them. Tom stepped forward and looked me sternly in the eyes. "You listen to me, Kiddo. It is just numbers on paper."

At the next trailhead a couple gave me a bag of pistachios. Then a younger couple overheard us and gave me a fresh mango.

People tell me all the time that the world is a terrible place full of dangerous people. Maybe they need to go hiking.

Ah! Wilderness

July 23, 2013

I was sitting against a tree for my lunch break, singing a little tune with my feet up on my backpack. Cracking open pistachios, I said out loud, "Man, this is a lot of work."

Then I burst out laughing.

Knowing my future held moments way less simple, in which I'd be stressed with my job, and wish with all my heart that I was sitting against a tree cracking open pistachios.

On a 40-mile day, sitting with my dinner feeling proud, I heard a loud crack and looked over to see a bear. She was about 30 feet away and looked just as surprised to see me as I was to see her. I yelled at her like she was a bad dog, "Go on! Get!" She disappeared quickly back into the trees. I felt like a jerk, but hopefully it protected her.

I've come to understand that running water is nature's most extraordinary gift. Whenever I get to take a break by a flowing stream, I feel I could stay forever. I understand that I belong in the woods. If I could convince my friends and family to live there with me, I would never leave.

I don't bother pitching tents anymore. I sleep out under the stars. It feels like the way I should have been sleeping all my life. Then sometimes I notice my moon shadow and fall asleep to Cat Stevens in my head. No one is ever really all that alone.

It's been hot, but hey, it's July. Tolerance is one of the best traits a person can have. There is no such thing as unacceptable. There's just everything that is, and how you handle it.

Birds of Prey

July 26, 2013

I've been thinking a lot about eagles. This may be a bit of a shock, but I don't like them. Many people admire their beauty, their magnificent wingspan, their grace...I think they're jerks. Please, hear me out though.

Eagles are bad news for the loons I study in Glacier National Park. In my hopes to see the population come back I've had a few heartbreaks in the death of loon chicks by eagle. Nature will be nature, and I don't question her plan. Sometimes I just don't like it.

Benjamin Franklin had a problem with the eagle being our nation's choice of representation. When I learned that, I agreed with him, though most of the students laughed and rolled their eyes. Ben said it was too aggressive and feared that it would set us down the wrong path as a young nation. I'm not crazy about the wild turkey he suggested, but that's just from personal experience. If it were up to me, I'd pick a bear or a horse. Something strong and peaceful, to remind us of freedom.

Last spring, on a road trip through northern California and Oregon, I noticed a reoccurring scene. I would often see a small bird intensely chasing a crow. Whenever I saw it, I would say, "You show 'em, little bird." A week or two later, we returned to Whitefish, Montana. I went for a run around the outskirts, by a farm, where I saw it again; a feisty songbird chasing away a crow. This time I was close enough to realize that the crow had one of the little bird's babies in its mouth. We see what we want to see. And it's not about right or wrong.

I'm bringing this up, because I want to clarify that I'm aware of such birds. I am sort of like a squirrel. Lately, a few strangers and loved ones have expressed concern that I'm too positive, unrealistic even. I think squirrels are fully aware of hawks and falcons. How do you go about being a squirrel in a world where something could swoop down from the sky?

You hop. You climb. You don't miss the flower patches. For it's better to risk the great, wide open than to live your life hiding in the trees.

My dear friends and family, thank you for your concern. I don't need a knife, I certainly don't need a gun, and I don't need to be reminded that I'm vulnerable. I just need you all to sit back and watch me go.

I owe a huge thank you to those of you who have shown faith in me. Especially to my parents. Thank you for believing in me.

Be Where Your Feet Are

August 12, 2013

Have you ever been in a place in life where you want to remember every second? How it smells, how your body feels, how you reason, your emotions, the taste of the air, the spring in your step? The love.

All my relationships have grown into something deeper.

Ooooofta. Where to begin?

I'm nearing the home stretch, and I'm glad to say that I'm sad to realize it.

In Oregon, the beer is hoppy, the locals are healthy and smiley, dogs are everywhere, the trail is flat and stunning, and generosity seems to be springing out of the ground.

Beads and I hiked 209 miles in seven days. For beer.

Bend, Oregon is known for its microbreweries, and there's something about a hoppy IPA that seems to dangle like a carrot on the horse track. When she and I realized that all we had to do was hike 30 miles a day for 5 days to make it to town for a Saturday night pub crawl, it was a done deal.

Then, guess what? We suck-diddly-ucked at pub crawling. We ended up only hitting two breweries before we started tipping over into our frothy pint glasses. Turns out physical exhaustion doesn't pair well with beer flights. It was the journey to beer town, not the destination.

Of course, there's more. There's always more. But for now, I want to be where my feet are. Which is in the home of two trail angels. I've been in Portland for the weekend and given gems and riches beyond my imagination. Feeling full and steady.

Long may we walk.

Contrast

August 17, 2013

Many hikers opt to walk 40 miles in one day on their way into Timberline Lodge. Other than the climb up Mt. Hood at the end, it's referred to as the easiest stretch on the trail. What better time to push it than when you end at a restaurant?

Yet, I found myself in times of trouble, walking up sinking dunes at 9pm with wind whipping sand and cold rain in my eyes. From what I could make out in twilight, I was on a sandy ridge with drop-offs on either side. When I thought 'Timberline' I pictured a heavily forested wonderland with a lodge made of gigantic logs. Turns out that Timberline represents what I call "tree line".

I could work on making less assumptions.

I ended up tucked between low trees in a tent just before the big, bright light in the distance that I assumed was the hotel. I pitched quickly and scooted out of the rain and wind to the safe-haven of my tent. I was determined to make my own meal before heading to the bar. That way I would spend less money, maybe even wait till morning to visit the hotel. From the straw of my reserve, I squeezed the rest of my water into my pot. It came up a few inches from its base. "Not enough. Well, well. What a lovely excuse to stumble into the bar."

Stumble indeed. I tripped down a minor rockslide, stepped through an unexpected creek, and shuffled like a zombie toward the bright light. And there it was, glowing with warmth and welcome. The Timberline Lodge.

From raging winds, sand, sharp rain pelting my face, and the roar of wild water came silence. And remarkable warmth. Peace. It hit me like a wave when I opened the glass side door.

Several heads lifted from books in wooden rocking chairs. I beamed back heartedly, though my senses were confused, and it was obvious that I was a curious sight.

Soon, I understood why. I went into the ladies' room and jumped back from the figure staring back at me in the mirror. "That's what I look like?" My hair was frayed in every direction, my face and teeth speckled with sand, my eyes narrow and blood shot.

Warm water pouring out of sinks is a fascinating thing. Not only is it warm but it comes without any flying elements. I got to work wetting my frayed hairs and removing the sandy layers from my skin.

After that I made my way to the upstairs bar. It was a unique space, a hexagon-shaped balcony with unmatched furniture tucked in cubbies. The glow of liquor bottles with neon lights behind them were on the opposite side of the circle.

I limped up to the bartender and ordered one of the tastiest beers I've ever had, a local IPA from Hood River. I made friends with the man next to me. By the bottom of my glass we were both teary eyed, dreaming about a simple cabin in the woods, doing what we love all the time. Poverty with a view, like Montana.

A bread bowl of vegetarian chili and a stumble back to my tent made for a fabulous collapse. I vowed to come back here someday. Maybe even climb Mt. Hood. But first, sleep.

Shrek's Swamp

August 21, 2013

I spent last night in a treehouse in a whimsical place known as Shrek's Swamp. A friendly trail angel has transformed his yard into multi-layers of structures, including tent pads, the tree house which will someday be multilevel, and coming soon, a hobbit dome.

I spent the evening with the presence of cartoon Donkey in my head, but there were many brilliant others. Especially Let It Be, a humble man who's working on his quadruple triple crown. You get the triple crown from hiking the PCT, AT, and CDT all the way through. I hope to get mine in 2015 after completing the Continental Divide Trail, the next big adventure.

Hikers teased me by the fire that night for my fear of the walk across the Bridge of the Gods. It's a PCT landmark, crossing the Columbia River from Oregon into Washington. I've never been good with heights, especially structures one can see through like fire towers and bridges. Meanwhile, there's not much room for walkers beside rushing cars.

The next morning, I was slightly uncomfortable walking the bridge, but I made it. I'm grateful to be in one piece and in the third and final state of the PCT. I might as well have entered it with a bang.

The Color of Wet

September 7, 2013

I know what you're going to say.

YOU: How's your hike going?

ME: It's been good. I'm feeling a little cheated by the weather habits though. I think out of my 18 days in Washington, 13 were rainy.

YOU: Yeah. And?

ME: Well, it sucks to be in that much rain.

YOU: Sure. However, it's Washington. What did you expect?

ME: Less than 13 days of rain.

YOU: Didn't you used to live in Washington?

ME: Yes, but this is SUPPOSED to be the dry time.

YOU: I see. Seems funny to hear someone who knows Washington being surprised about the rain.

ME: I suppose it does.

YOU: Yup. (Long awkward silence). You should eat something.

That sums up my sentiments. All the hikers I've seen lately have been soaked and commiserating like champions. The water in my shoes makes a squeaking rhythm that spices up my musical scores as I walk. The views pop out of the clouds on occasion.

I'm poking a lot of fun at this, yet my spirits stayed high. I've had three rainy days on the whole trail until Washington, which is kid stuff compared to the A.T. And besides, if you're going to move to the woods for the summer, you might encounter some moisture.

Here's a list of some songs that rain will make you think of:

Rain Drops Keep Falling on My Head

Singing in the Rain

Rain Rain Go Away

Rainy Days and Mondays

Reign on Me

Kiss the Rain

Unwritten (Feel the Rain on Your Skin)

River in the Rain

And, if you're lucky, The Rainbow Connection

I met Eric at Steven's Pass. After about a week and a half of soggy walking, I crawled out of the woods to his smiling face waiting at the trail head. We went to Seattle for a long weekend, visited his family, saw a few of my most wonderful friends, walked around the city, and thought we'd enjoy the sunny weekend in town. That way we could return to the trail with the return of rain.

Eric hiked 17 miles his first day, then 21, then 24, passing several rained-out hikers in their tents at 4:30 the last evening. The next morning, he woke me up, started my stove, opened the valve to let the air out of my sleeping pad and said, "Let's get moving." while I was asking for five more minutes.

So, his trail name is Gofer. Which is twofold, with him being incredibly Minnesotan and his surprising ability to go for it.

When the sun came out, we had a "yard sale," spreading everything we had in the sweet, sweet sunshine to get the color of wet out of it.

At the end of a 19-mile downhill day, we dropped into a town called Stehekin. Just in time for the 6:15 bus to the last, best town on the trail.

It might not have been evident in my blogs, but by this time in the hike, I couldn't make sense of anything but the woods. Which is why I clung with every toe and finger to my last couple of weeks. There was shocking news from my family. A wordless battle scrambled into form which I didn't understand myself, let alone have the ability to translate for others.

Basket-Case

September 11, 2013

The trail can be a bit demanding from time to time. It makes for some interesting emotional responses. I've been in circles of hikers where even the tough could admit to suddenly bursting into tears. These outbursts come unannounced and at a steady flow. It could be because you saw something beautiful and felt grateful, or you thought of something sad, or felt so tired you couldn't stand it, or got lost (my personal best hissy-fit). It could be for no reason at all. This comes with the territory.

I took it up a notch this week with the news that my big sister, Brea, has cancer. I found myself at a whole new level of insanity.

For example, one morning Eric and I came to a flowing stream and sat down. As I dipped my water bottle into its current, I thought how much I was going to miss getting water that way. How I love the sound of the rushing creek. How I know there are tough realities waiting for me back home and I wish I could stay.

The river began to sing to me. *Stay with me.*

Eric walked off, and I followed reluctantly, staying far behind him so that he couldn't hear my whimpering.

At times, I've been extremely positive. When the sun comes out, I scan the horizon with tingles in my skin, then whisper to myself, "Take it all in. You're so lucky to be able to have this." When the rain gets heavy, I think, "There's nothing to complain about. You get to be healthy."

I came to a log too big to climb over. Eric found his way around after a bit of difficulty, as I sat down in the branches. "Just leave me here."

His puzzled look helped me realize how unreasonable I must have seemed. But in my head was a screaming child saying, "I can't get over this log and my sister has cancer." If not for him, who knows how long I would have cried there.

In Stehekin, I struggled to gather information from home using the one payphone in town. Its connection was shaky, having just been hit that week by a mudslide. All I could hear my dad say was that Brea starts chemo tomorrow. It was more serious than I'd thought.

Stehekin is only accessible by boat or foot, which makes it a lovely place to be, though a tough place to quickly exit. I approached two women I had met that morning while they were eating their breakfast in town. They were visiting their brother, Chief, one of my hiking friends. The only place to go was to my family. These two women would know details on transportation.

I ended up bawling into both of their chests, grateful for the comfort of women. One of them cried with me. The whole restaurant kept looking toward us, pretending not to mind that there was a hysterical young woman ruining their breakfast. You gotta do what you gotta do.

I settled down a bit and asked the woman behind the store counter if I could use a phone for a family emergency. She asked no questions, dialed the number for me, and I got to have a reasonable conversation with my dad. He told me sternly to finish the trail. Then he had my brother-in-law call to fill me in.

Brea had Ewing's Sarcoma. An aggressive cancer of the blood, fat, or tissue. She was prescribed 12 weeks of chemotherapy, then surgery to remove the tumor on her collar bone, then 22 more weeks of chemo. We'd be going through this for a year. My parents and siblings were all gathered in the hospital, insisting that I finish the hike.

I spent a couple of days not moving in Stehekin, one of the most beautiful towns I've ever seen. I swam in Lake Chelan, asking the water to help me live and feel. Then we moved on, heavy-hearted but extra grateful. With 88 miles to go.

The Home Stretch

September 17, 2013

Stehekin is what America was, they say. People were truly relaxing. No gadgets, no glazed faces staring into screens, just bones in hammocks, chairs, or on the grass. People sinking into the ground properly with eyes closed and a light smile across their lips.

The teal waters of Lake Chelan calmed my nervous system. We pitched a tent next to the lake. The stars were luminous. As I took in the still of the night, I became desperate to hold on to it forever. I bargained with Eric. "What if I didn't have any bills. What if I got rid of my car and my cell phone and paid off my student loans and owned nothing so I didn't need storage. Then can I stay?"

He seemed scared to hear it. Maybe he's worried about my emotional health. Or me fitting back into society. Maybe he's afraid I'll run amuck, take off my clothes, and build a campfire in the middle of downtown Steamboat this winter while dancing around shouting, "People. You need to listen to the trees."

I can't promise that won't happen.

I walked the next three days with Eric in a skewed reality. The plants and rocks meant more to me, though they didn't seem real.

An older gentleman set up a camp for hikers at Hart's Pass. I sat there with a veggie burger on my lap and a glass full of whiskey and root beer between my fingers. I breathed in the warmth of the scene like it was medicine. A special kind of magic, simply knowing that people want to be there for each other. Meander was the name of the host. And several hikers had made it to the Canadian border and hiked back to Hart's Pass. Champagne bottles were being passed around and Meander told stories about hiking across New Zealand. Which is on my agenda.

On our last night, we camped on a grassy ridge. Shades of blazing orange and red reflected off the great rock wall surrounding us. The last sunset on trail. I stayed out staring at it long after Eric turned in, journaling unproductively. Not at all sure what was in my head.

The next day was an easy hike to the border. My friend, Chief, caught up to us. We were lost in conversation until the clear-cut line in the trees, known as the 49th Parallel, shocked me. My heart pounded. My stomach lurched. For some reason it was spooky, like a ghost.

We stood at the northern terminus moments later. It was 12:01 pm, September 15th, and the trail was over. I'm still not sure I have words for it.

Kicking and Screaming

September 28, 2013

I'm back in the world now. Trying to make it fit. Trying to keep the wild in my eyes and the peace in my heart. Trying not to cry.

I think of nature. Not the woods specifically, not the mountain either, but all of it. The big Everything. I hope that I can hold on to it. Take it with me.

So little needs to be explained in the woods. I don't have an urge to make anything at all understood. How refreshing that has been. How well taken care of I've felt. At home. I have no words for so many of the things I felt out there, or the things I feel now. How can you be a human without needing to be understood?

Next to the raging waters, I felt loved. Against the trees, accepted. Respected by the other creatures.

It's not that I need people less, it's more than ever. Friends, family, and strangers alike. I can't feel anything but love for them. I wish I could share what I've gained in a way that they could gain it too.

I don't want life to be any less profound than it feels right now. I'm scared. Not of being unimportant, but of assigning things the wrong importance.

I'm fearful of closing in any way. I'm full of dread for the misunderstandings. I miss the trail.

Great Expectations

October 2, 2013

I've been trying to boil my walk down to a life lesson. Hoping to learn what the universe is avidly attempting to teach me. I think it's about expectations.

Countless times, I've ruined things for myself by expecting too much of something before it happens. Other times, I've found connection and gratitude for being alive by letting everything go. By waking up in the morning and feeling thankful, since waking up each morning is not a guarantee.

Each town I heard of set a precedent in my mind. People would rave about upcoming locations and then I would get there expecting to be blown away. It would turn out to be a quiet town and the brewery a humble cafe with beer, and because I was anticipating more, I'd feel let down. Then, if I should expect little, if other hikers and locals were saying, "Good luck with that one," or "Don't hold your breath," I would be pleasantly surprised.

I compared the AT to the PCT. I don't want to do that anymore. This was my second thru-hike. I showed up a different way. My friends and family did, too. California, Oregon, and Washington are nothing like Appalachia. An orange is nothing like an apple. Why would you ever hold something in your hands and think about what it isn't?

Cheryl Strayed wrote *Wild* about a hike on the PCT. People in the hiking community are spitfirey because "She didn't really hike the trail." Her book is not about thru-hiking. It's a raw and honest account of what she went through in coping with her mother's sudden death. If you have to hold her up to your own set of standards before spending time with her words, you're missing out. You could have learned something beautiful.

I walked for months dreaming of the end. Of walking into my old restaurant in Seattle and saying, "Caminé desde México," to my Mexican friends.

That's not what happened. I stood at the Canadian border feeling unmoved, yet appreciative, then rushed to Minnesota. There are so many things in life you won't see coming. Like your sister's cancer diagnosis at age 29, for example.

But truly, that's life. To bleed is real, and I won't be able to do so when I'm gone. I know the answer to each moment must be yes. I know I can't expect the sun to go on shining or my legs to go on walking. So, I've got to be grateful. As often as I can think to, be lucky, be blessed, and notice my wealth.

Continental Divide Trail 2015

3,000-ish Miles

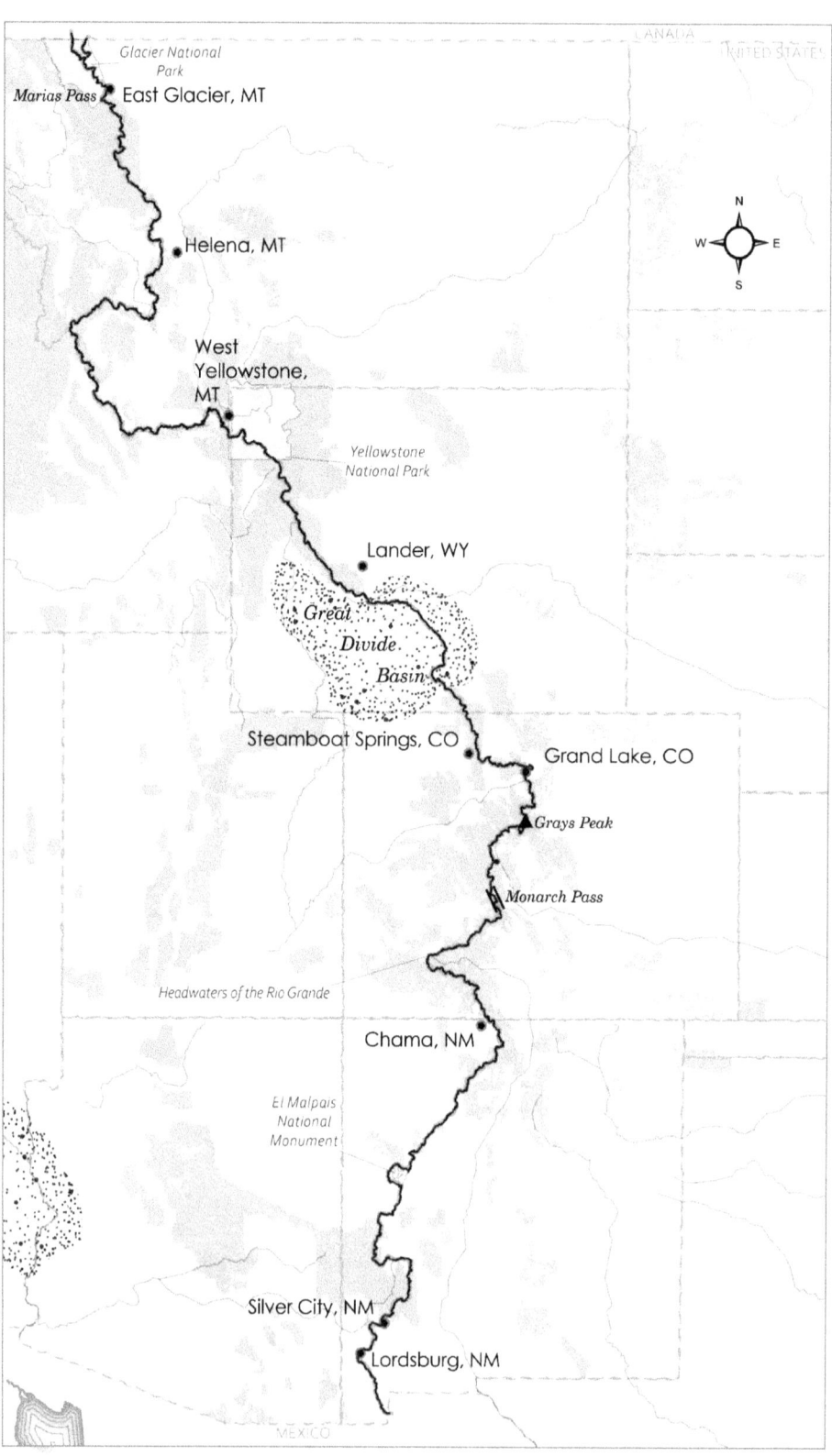

A benefit to getting older is that I get worse at hiding my truth as the years go by. As though I was born with a ration of sugar to coat myself. The hail and cold rain made quick work of whatever sweetener was left on the divide.

Winter of 2013/2014 was a grueling season of restaurant work, family hardships, and training for an ultramarathon. A winter that Eric and I couldn't make it through. We parted as friends in Steamboat Springs at the end of ski season, and I moved back to Montana.

The training I did to get my body conditioned for distance running became my deepest companion for a summer of passionate wonder. I got to know Glacier National Park in a new way, running through its rugged trails, collecting obscure locations like a cult fan.

I was that. I'd been in love with Glacier since I was 14 and landing there to root myself in its wildflowers was extremely effective medicine after a year of hospital visits and broken hearts. All I wanted was wilderness. Not nicely maintained trails with endearing brown signs. I wanted devil's club to abrade my thighs and cow parsnip so overgrown that I got it in my eyes. I showed up to work with sticks in my hair and stories about falling into tree wells or getting washed downstream.

Many stories I kept to myself. Out-of-body experiences had both grounded and expanded me. Whatever I came to understand about myself being holy, came also with the acceptance that I was equal parts messy. I became chaos. And I became the void.

I spent the following winter songwriting and nannying two wild boys for a family in Columbia Falls. My family woes settled as we learned more about supporting my brother and my sister made it to remission from her cancer treatment. I waitressed and bartended to save money. Then I went walking the Continental Divide. No GPS. No partner to check in with. No idea what was going to happen.

About

March 14, 2015

I'm setting out on a walkabout from Mexico to Canada, which stretches along the spine of our continent, along the magnificent Rocky Mountains. Someone is going to drop me off on the Mexican border, and I'm going to spend my summer walking home. A dream for me that's getting more real by the moment.

I'll have my fair share of challenges, I'm sure. The Continental Divide Trail is seldom marked and offers several different route options. I'll be navigating the whole trek with maps and a compass, which means I'll likely spend a decent amount of my time lost. The CDT is known for extreme weather, be it wind, hail, or afternoon electrical storms when the nearest tree is 3,000 feet below you. There are hundreds of miles of desert and the Great Basin to cross. As well as steep, deep snow to traverse in the Colorado Rockies.

The journey starts April 21st, with hopes to return to Glacier before the Sperry Chalet closes on September 9th. Sperry is my happy place, a mountain chalet six miles into the backcountry. People reserve rooms there to spend the night and enjoy hiking the most beautiful scenery I know. When I'm spending summers in Glacier, I go up to the chalet once a week and bring fresh fruit to the staff. The views are amazing, but I'm equally attracted to the hot sandwiches I get to sit down to. It's my goal to hike to one of those sandwiches this summer.

It is truly an honor to be able to live this way. I treasure the support I receive and the opportunities I've been blessed with. I'll do my best to share it.

I will have mail drops along the way. It's touching to be thought of, and I'm always hungry. Just last week, I was sitting at Apgar Lookout with my friend Dan, taking in the beautiful snow-covered skyline of Glacier's western peaks, feeling alive and lucky. I looked over to him and said, "Do you want to know what hiking's really about?"

He straightened his shoulders and perked up his ear.

I pulled a burrito and a bag of kettle chips out of my backpack and grinned. "Eating. It's about eating."

The Beginning

March 16, 2015

It's time. The earth is coming out and the air is alive with moisture. Some things are about to grow. I hope to be one of them. If I should be so lucky. To change with the seasons, to run with the water, to bloom with the flowers would be so simple and so tremendous at the same time. The deeper I go into these woods, the better my chances.

I keep thinking of the phrase *give up*. Not sure in what sense. To give up comfort, maybe. At least to a certain degree. To give up explanations for a little while and give silence the right of way. Or to stop fighting. To not extend or contort or work to manipulate anything. Just to be.

Thank you to all my loved ones for your support. If love didn't walk with me, I never would have gotten anywhere. Let's go on this journey and see what it has to teach us.

Lessons in Length

April 4, 2015

Last weekend I went running in Moab, Utah, with a few of my closest friends and my father there to support me. Distance running has become my teacher, bringing lessons like the importance of giving up control. I can make something happen for myself. I can save up enough money to move to NYC as a teenager or put together enough food to get from Georgia to Maine. But I can't plan for the choices made in the moment or the thunderheads coming in hot.

And speaking of coming in hot, the high for the race was 87 degrees. My last words to Shasta as I left the hotel room at 5 in morning were, "I'm not carrying a backpack. Backpacks are for suckers." We all laughed as I gave her a kiss on the cheek.

Flash forward to 2:30pm, mile 38, and you can find me belly up in the shade of a short, twisted tree. "This is a good day to die," I said to myself as I covered my limbs with dirt and then watched a montage of loving faces flash before my eyes.

I left the checkpoint at mile 33 with a hoot. My dad and Shasta and a few other spectators cheered back as I scrambled up to the ridge. Three miles later, I looked down at my handheld water bottle. "Eight miles to the next check point," I heard the nice woman from mile 33 say. Then it hit me. I had five ounces of water left in my one bottle. Five miles to go. In what world did I think one 16-ounce water bottle was all that I needed? My watch read 2pm and the sun seemed menacing.

I'll just run fast. My body feels strong, and the water will come sooner.

For the longest 10 minutes of my life, I ran as fast as I could stand to and kept glancing at my watch. Time must have been playing some kind of cruel trick. Every spurt of energy I expended seemed not to register on the clockface. Before long, I realized I'd fried myself. I couldn't walk in a straight line and felt a throbbing in my head. My fingers and toes tingled.

That's when I lay down to die. I don't think it was all delirium, probably some, but if it was my time to go, I wanted to do it well. So, I sat down under a hunched tree and began to cover my skin with handfuls of loose dirt. "Turn me back into dust," I said. I opened my heart and poured dirt all over it.

Another racer came by, a woman I had run a mile or two with a few hours before. She wanted me to walk four miles with her to the next aid station. I tried, but zig-zagged too much, then picked another tree and insisted she move on. She offered to split the little water she had left, and I refused. Everyone needed it desperately.

I ate a Luna Bar. To my surprise, it helped a great deal. Ten minutes later I was able to walk. While slowly pacing my way, a man on a dirt bike came by. I flagged him down and explained my predicament. He gave me all the water he had and introduced himself as Isaac. Saying, "I know I'm on one of these, but I'm actually an endurance athlete too. I've gotten myself in the same situations, trying to carry as little as possible."

I ran a bit, but mostly walked to the finish line. My barefoot dad and dear friend, Heidi, ran beside me.

A special thanks to mother nature for the backhand smack that I truly needed. I'm going to pay close attention to what I carry on the CDT. Especially the water.

Saying Goodbye

April 12, 2015

It's my last night in Montana. I said goodbye to my cat this morning and went home to my empty cabin to clean it. I couldn't stop thinking about the closing of this current chapter. How it's been a time for growth, which doesn't always feel lovely, but it's always worth going through, and I'm grateful.

On my last day as nanny for two delightful, wild boys, we set up tent city in the yard. We agreed that it was the coolest thing the three of us had ever done together. Some friends came to play with us. Three women and four children huddled in the same two-person tent.

Tomorrow, I set out. In some ways it feels like my steps on to the platform at the train station are the most significant. The real beginning. Though where the journey actually begins, I can never seem to say. I think it already has.

Oh, Montana. I leave you again, but this time I'm crossing you in style. Goodbye dear friends, I'll see you always.

Home to Home

April 21, 2015

I'm here. My trail brother from the AT, Stephen, is here too. He plans to hike the first few hundred miles. We flew into Flagstaff, AZ to stay with Sara-Tide (my non-hiking name for her), the other member of our family. Stephen and I took a Greyhound from there to Lordsburg, NM, which is the launching pad for the start of the hike.

I haven't stopped grinning since. A PCT buddy, Cookie Monster, was on the register at the front desk of our hotel. I went to his room for "*hiker happy hour*" and we told stories of the time we were once short-sighted enough to hike 30+ miles in the San Jacinto Mountains without any warm gear in cold rain and sleet. Good times.

Our shuttle to the bootheel of New Mexico departs at 6:15 tomorrow morning. In previous hikes I've taken this moment to spell out some expectations to laugh at later. This time, it doesn't feel right. If nothing else, I've learned to uproot expectations.

On my bus ride here, I read John Steinbeck's *Travels with Charley*. There was a beautiful quote to fit the scenery.

Life could not change the sun, or water the desert, so it changed itself.

I remember the jitters of the last couple of hikes. The teary goodbyes. The weight. This time it's just love. I told the circle of friends today that I was feeling glad to be around other thru-hikers. To finally not be the weirdo with the obscure desire.

Cookie Monster and the others raised their beers for a toast and said, "Welcome home."

Just Don't Step on a Cactus

April 25, 2015

I've made it through the first 100 miles back to Lordsburg. Great but not graceful. I have a racoon sunburn on my face, a little stiffness in my legs, hunger enough for three people, and joy. It feels great to be back at it.

I spent most of my time alone, wanting to gauge my navigation skills and check in with myself. The CDT is truly not a trail all the time. Sometimes it's wide-open terrain marked by piles of rocks called cairns or poles sticking out of the ground. At times I can't see the next post and get a slight sense of gravity in my gut, searching for the smartest next move. But if I keep walking and trusting the general direction something reveals itself five minutes later.

I'm loving the desert more and more. Hard to believe as a creature of the north. I appreciate wide open views. The plants, the dirt, and most of all, the reptiles. What troopers. I almost stepped on a horny toad the other day and could swear I heard it say, "Blend in," like in the movie *Rango*. I saw two snakes sprawled across the dirt, soaking up sunlight. I thought about the 30-pound bag on my back, full of things to eat and items to protect me from the sun. And there they were, exposed.

That's the word. Exposed. That's what turns out to feel heavy about the desert. You *have* to live with it. There is nothing else. When the rain comes, when the sun is hot, the trees aren't there to save you.

It feels cunning in a way. Learning something important about what's in me instead of what's out there for me.

Stormy Weather

April 28, 2015

Silver City, New Mexico. A place with southwestern style, burritos on every corner, coffee, beer, and friendly locals. Basically, an oasis for hikers thru and through. I'm here with Stephen, Jay (a hiker from DC) and G-Funk (a hiker from Austria) who were both dropped off at the start of the trail in the same shuttle I boarded seven days ago.

In one week, we've been scorched and snowed on. Lost and lonesome. Hungry and happy. A perfect slice of trail life. I've been telling my family and friends that, so far, what I love most about this trail is its intensity. Because of it, I feel like we're a similarly focused bunch of individuals. In past thru-hikes, the start feels more like a party. This time, it feels like a back-country experience.

Two days ago, I woke up next to a windmill with Jay and Stephen. We got moving early. It started to rain, and then within the hour, snow. We were wet and cold and thinking it was going to be one of those days where we eat a walking lunch of protein bars and packet snacks to keep moving and stay warm. Then out of the trees emerged a dilapidated shelter. Or half of one. The way we all jumped for joy we could have been mistaken for kids going to Disneyland.

Five hikers were huddled inside. We shivered together and told stories of previous trails for three hours, until the rain and sleet let up. Then we hiked on through the Gila National Forest topped with an inch of snow. And the sun came out.

That's what thru-hiking has given me. Gratitude. Copious amounts of it for things like warm cups of coffee and rusty old structures, and, more than anything, the people to shiver with.

So Very Lost

May 6, 2015

Over the last few months, I've joked about the ins and outs of navigation. Laughing off the heaviness of how being misplaced is just part of the experience. I had a great opportunity to practice that acceptance.

For the majority of the last week, I've been in the Gila National Forest. Walking a river canyon with native dwellings, caves, sheer cliffs, and a whole lot of water. The river's turquoise surfaces have kept me mesmerized. Enough to hardly notice the work involved with fording the same river over 150 times, which taxes the body, whether your high spirits notice or not.

One night, I came to a relaxing hot spring filled with laughing families. The water felt great and the company even more so, but for reasons I can only chalk up to my German blood, I moved on. It was 6:30. I wanted to put in another couple of miles before dark. As I walked away, I got this strange feeling I was making a mistake, but I didn't stop. I witnessed my behavior with curiosity. *I am opting to spend the night alone, away from laughter and comfort, just to get in another mile or two.*

I woke up the next morning, pushed a little over 20 miles without seeing a soul, slept, got up, and pushed again. Still no sign of another hiker. Around 2 in the afternoon, I was starting to get a little weary and uneasy. I found myself scrambling in a box canyon, trying to keep three points of contact on steep rock while the river gushed below. I felt the tug of Samwise (my backpack) pulling me backward as I gripped the fragmented rock. "They told me you were brutal, CDT, but I wasn't expecting this."

I'd been expecting the river to join Snow Lake for hours. Instead, it became more of a creek. I tried a side trail to get up high and see if I could catch a glimpse of the lake. There was nothing even remotely like one. I came back down and carried on a bit more, then got out my compass (what a concept) and saw that I was traveling rather in the direction of south. It was then that I realized I was not where I was supposed to be. And not knowing when I got off course, I figured I had walked right off my maps.

A range of emotions came into play, disappointment in myself being the predominant. Then the *I-want-my-mommy* feeling. Then acceptance.

I asked for time alone and the growth of getting lost in the woods. Wish granted.

I turned around. Walked for the rest of the day hoping to get back to where I went wrong. Eventually I would either find a confluence I'd missed or another hiker.

Twelve miles later, after a shady scramble down the same crumbling slot canyon, I figured it out. The night before I had been exhausted and stumbling through the bushes trying to find a decent place to step on the bank of the river, and I didn't even notice that a lovely little tributary, Iron Creek, had joined us. Rather, I joined it. For a full day.

I followed every turn in the river religiously from then on, with my poles stashed, map in hand, and compass around my neck. I navigated. As I should have been doing the whole time I was on the river. I got lazy, thinking all I had to do was follow the water's path. Paid for it. Learned from it. Then was given the opportunity to apply it to life experience.

The next group of hikers I came to, I stuck with. Brett, Butters, and Page. Page is driving a camper-truck to meet them and camp with them and their three dogs. We've been joking and telling each other stories about our homelands. It's better together.

Pie and Presence

May 13, 2015

There's a town in New Mexico that's named for its pie. What a lovely concept. I'd love to live in Cinnamon Roll City, or Cookieville, or West Danish. This place is called Pie Town. There are about 60 people living here, and they treat the hikers like family. You can stay at Nita's Toaster House if you're a weary traveler. Nita was not there, but her neighbors keep the fridge stocked and you can crash anywhere there is space to lie down.

I was planning to spend only one night, then I woke up sick in my sleep. I think it was something I ate. The next morning, I felt a bit nauseous and still thought it was a good idea to be heading out that afternoon. I'm like that.

Then my old friend from the PCT, Thirsty Boots, arrived. I had no idea he was on the trail this year. I consider him one of my dearest hiking friends and have even visited his home and family in Vermont. We caught up and ended up playing old Appalachian tunes with resident guitars that evening.

I took a lot of naps that day. Hikers patted me on the head and wished me well. Cookie Monster brought me tea. I allowed the comforts, which was considerably better than sleeping alone in my tent.

By afternoon, I was ready for more pie. A friendly band of string players were singing some of my favorite songs in harmony. I forgot how much music can heal. I sat next to them and sang along. There was a banjo, a fiddle, and a guitar, with the occasional upright bass and mandolin added in.

Later that night, more hiking friends arrived. I sang an original tune that I had written about thru-hiking, *Water with a Pulse*. I felt heard in the crowd of faces as they sank into the couch cushions. Grateful to have connected. To have stayed.

New Mexico, You Magnificent Bastard

May 21, 2015

Marvelous New Mexico, what can I say? In one month, I've had more boat-rocking experiences than an entire summer in Glacier or my other two thru-hikes combined. I've never been hailed on so much or with so much gusto. Never crossed a river so many times. Never been lost so often. Never had to pitch my tent early in the evening to get out of the elements and woke up to crashes of thunder and a caved in tent with pounds of heavy snow. Never drank water quite that color. Never actually yelled, "That's enough!" at the wind and rain, like a pissed-off child.

I can't believe there's one state with all these things. From low desert to over 11,000 feet. You have reshaped me, New Mexico.

Thank you.

Thank you for the sun on the mesa. The painted rock, the turquoise water of the rushing stream, the cacti in bloom. Thank you for the many canyons connecting the way. The caves. The alpine. The humble towns opening to us dirty hikers. Thank you, thank you, thank you for the opportunities to get found. For leading me home and teaching me along the way.

I'm in Ghost Ranch tonight, milling about within rock structures and reflecting on my walk. In the last week, I've had it handed to me. Tonight, I'm dry, clean, and aware of being alive.

Flip-Flopping

May 26, 2015

Turns out, Colorado is snowy. Too snowy to feel comfortable walking through. It's 100% snowpack from here (Chama, NM) north, and that may last weeks. So, I've teamed up with a group of hikers to rent a vehicle and drive to central Wyoming, where we can hike the snow-free Great Basin. From there we will hike south. That puts us back here in six-to-seven weeks. Which will be a remarkable time to walk through the San Juan Mountains. There are loads of logistics to work out, but I'm getting it together. Happy, healthy, and ready for more adventure.

 Here's where we lost me. Driving past the state border signs in a car took away the romance of walking one line from Mexico to home. It felt like cheating. And I was already wondering if I believed in the mission.

Thirsty Boots and I had walked together for three days from Ghost Ranch to Chama. When we got to Chama, the trails were covered in feet of snow. Navigation proved even more challenging with buried road signs.

Another deep conversation with him illuminated how I was feeling about the trail. I didn't want it all that badly. Once the snow presented its obstacles, I couldn't help but wonder why I was doing it. I didn't need to prove to myself through suffering that I was worthy of love. I had felt loved beyond measurement by running wildly through the alpine of Montana.

On the snow there would be no naps in the grass or dips in mountain lakes. Flip-flopping was the obvious solution to getting out of the snow, but it compounded my loss of faith in the mission. None of it mattered, or more so, all of it mattered, but it didn't have to be anything specific. Why was I still hiking the Continental Divide Trail?

Basin, Great

June 2, 2015

Alas, I find myself in Rawlins, Wyoming. With a sunburn and a smile. We arrived in Lander five days ago, after seven of us crammed into a minivan and watched blankets of snow engulf the many tall peaks of Colorado. At times we were struck speechless, crossing our fingers that it may melt a bit while we're up here walking across the Great Basin.

And what a basin indeed. We crossed it in five days along the Oregon trail and California Cutoff. Our troupe was able to get a hitch in the back of a horse trailer, then blessed to experience good, clean walking. No blizzards or scary river crossings, though still some hail, as well as one active electric storm which had me crouching in a ditch yesterday.

The basin is green. Which is rare. This part of the trail is known for holding some of the longest stretches without water, but not this season. We've been told by ranchers that it's the wettest it ever gets. Which makes us quite lucky.

As do the inside jokes in the making and free-roaming pronghorns and wild horses.

Now we're off to sneak beer into a movie theater.

Montana Time

June 17, 2015

Another flip-flop, another set of laughs and unanticipated adventures. My hiking companions Banjo and Stabby, and I rented a car and drove to Helena, Montana to continue walking south. We are in Anaconda today. It feels great to be back in Montana, though I know I'll be walking out of it before too long. The snow proved to be an obstacle on the Wyoming/ Colorado border, but it's melted out here, almost entirely.

What I'm not telling the readers is that those decisions were painful and packed with questions. Was nature trying to tell me something about my attachment to a certain goal? Was my heart in it?

I told my hiking mates that I would only be willing to drive up as far as Helena. Saving Glacier for the end was important. What was more concerning is that if I ended up in Glacier in mid-summer, there was no way I would leave. My hike would end.

What an endearing thought, to end the hike and choose pleasure. Go back to the place I love most and live out a summer of trail runs like I'd had the year before. That would be the logical option, but would I ever forgive myself? I had planned this journey for years. People knew me as a thru-hiker. In many ways, I wasn't brave enough to abandon the mission. And there were rules.

Rules like connecting your footsteps. If you didn't walk every step of one continuous route, you wouldn't be a "real thru-hiker." And on our maps were paragraphs written by the cartographer that challenged hikers to pick the harder routes, saying we were there to be badass.

I didn't want to be badass. I wanted to be a woman. A sister. A lover. A daughter. In the gap between the PCT and CDT I had become obsessed with running long distances, even though it was painful on my lower back and hips. I was attached to it like it could save me, without knowing how or from what. My aunt Lu confronted me about it. I told her I needed to run to remind myself who I am.

Lu shook her head. "You've always been Shayla. You weren't always a runner."

In time I started to see what she meant. In Glacier I learned to surrender. That my body was strong and amazing, but that wasn't the point. The beauty around me was what was most important. Noticing it. Being with it. And telling it thank you for my health and freedom.

The men around me seemed to be fixated on loving themselves in nature. I was working to love the nature in myself.

Old Friends

June 27, 2015

How did I not know about the Pintlers? The ranges in the Beaverhead National Forest are truly incredible, glacier-sculpted and covered in wildflowers. The divide is prominent, and we walk its edge while looking out for many miles in all directions. This is the spine of the continent. Passing by Lewis and Clark waypoints and native battle fields.

I've been noticing that great Montana feel, sitting down for an occasional beer in town and talking to the locals. Everyone is what they are, in a beautiful way. I get opportunities to talk about the land with locals, the trails I've walked which they know and love. A special peace comes over them when they remember how much they love it. We laugh, we toast, and we feel connected, because we are.

Jesse is here to visit today. We were partners for eight years. Now we celebrate a concrete friendship that we can both rely on. He's the greatest link I have to who I am, other than my family. We stayed up talking and playing cards till 2 am last night. He's hiking out with me today.

I'm grateful.

Strange Magic

July 10, 2015

The last few weeks have been rough. I was wondering why, but then I did the math—500 miles in three weeks on steep, unmaintained trails. My struggles are rooted in physical strain. The bugs are doing what they do this time of year. The heat is rather intense. Meanwhile, me and the guys have been pushing 27-mile days and it's been wearing on me.

It all came crashing down in the usual five-year-old way when I called my mother. I was threatening to quit, saying that I don't know why I do this and that I feel irresponsible for leaving Max behind and needing so much help from my friends and family to keep this journey continuing. Adventure is losing its importance. Family matters more. Love matters more. So how can I keep doing this, when I know it doesn't really matter?

I told the guys I needed a day off in West Yellowstone. We hitched in for the 4th of July, enjoyed copious amounts of pizza, and heard fireworks through the night. Then I arranged a slack pack the next day, which allowed me to hike without the pain.

I had some incredible chance meetings in West Yellowstone that reminded me of the passion behind this, particularly a trail runner with a sparkle in his eyes. He was so excited for what I was up to that it reminded me how I feel about it. Which is lucky.

Then I let myself be still and focus on what's underneath it all.

We carried on into Yellowstone National Park. Then split up at Old Faithful, while I awaited my guaranteed package of new shoes at the post office. It's possible that much of my crappy attitude came from walking over 1,400 miles in the same pair of Keens.

The package did not come, despite the guarantee. The guys already left, thinking I'd be hiking out behind them this evening. They are probably worried, but I know I'll catch them in Dubois.

I was allowed to stay in employee housing here at the lodge. I never dreamed there would be a way to drop in to one of the most popular attractions in America and get a room for five bucks. I was given meal tickets by other employees, met some great adventurers and talked trails a bit. This experience reminds me who I am.

I was treated to dinner by a traveling couple. We had wine by the piano after dinner and played guess that tune. Another reminder of my background.

The pianist invited me to sing Joni Mitchell songs next to her.

After the greatest sleep of my trail so far, I feel charged and inspired. All these delays are teaching me some important things. Let it go. Trust. Be grateful. The rest will come.

The next day, I was faced with a decision. After a hitchhiking mishap where I lost my rain jacket (always keep your gear consolidated in a vehicle) I considered my options. I had three days before meeting the guys in Dubois. I could go into the woods of a remote corner of Yellowstone, the Beckler, without the proper gear and hustle to catch them. Or I could hitch into the Tetons and enjoy the kind of hiking I love most, long day journeys through alpine meadows and tarns (glaciated, high alpine lakes), then hitchhike to meet them.

I gazed longingly down US highway 89 toward the south, yet kept my thumb at my side. Part of me was joyfully jumping at the perfect excuse to give up on the mission. The other part of me was deeply contemplating the gravity of such a choice. I decided not to decide for the time-being and walked eight miles to my reserved campsite.

In my tent I stared at the maps. The upcoming section was known for being the most remote in the county; the farthest one could get from any road in the lower 48. It would have been less than wise to go anywhere in the Rockies without a good rain jacket, let alone that section. After leaving the park boundary was a stretch nicknamed "the horse (poop) superhighway." Which only sounded so appealing. The more I looked at the maps and milage the less I knew.

As I rolled over and listened to the quiet Yellowstone night, I heard what I needed to hear. My heart.

Choose joy.

The next morning I hiked the eight miles back to the highway and found a friend immediately. Paul, from Indiana, was enjoying photography opportunities and open for company. He took me to the hiker/biker section of the same campground he was staying at. I met a web of traveling humans, biking and hiking across the country. There was joy, just like that.

I took a shuttle bus to trailheads and went on two 25-mile day hikes in glorious backcountry. In the evening, over camping meals at a picnic table, Paul and I talked about our days. Before long we were opening deeply, expressing our connection to nature and that which some may call God, though I wasn't one to do so. Paul was a pastor of a small congregation. One of his children had been through a gender transition. He smiled when he told me how proud he was. Grateful to be an example through his congregation of how easy it is to love.

When I hitchhiked from the Tetons to Dubois the next day, I felt a freedom I hadn't yet known. I had sabotaged my triple crown. And it was bliss. I wasn't hiking for a crown. I was hiking for my spirit. I was peering into nature, rather than looking at it. I was answering myself.

Running, Water, and Running Water

July 21, 2015

There aren't many experienced hikers in the Mountain West who don't get all dreamy-eyed when you mention the Wind Rivers. Now I see why. Dramatic peaks, scrambles over talus and boulder fields, spectacular cirques with bright blue waters, and valleys and parks nestled so comfortably in the colored rock. I hope to encourage everyone who's willing to get there someday.

I made the brilliant decision that I didn't need a rain jacket for this past week of travel. And paid for it. I ended up pitching my tent midday to keep warm. A first for me. It was cold rain, nothing I've never seen, but perhaps I've taken for granted how much the gear saves my life. I've joked about the game I like to play called *keep-moving-or-die*, but this time it didn't seem like the wisest game to play. It's good to be getting older.

Banjo and I were both sporting handsome, yellow, vinyl ponchos, the likes of which you can obtain from your local gas station for $2.49. Banjo and I were unprepared.

He passed me in my tent. I told him I would be fine after warming up for an hour or two and he tentatively walked on, hoping to keep moving and stay warm. Half an hour later I heard his footsteps return, "Kiddo, I'm being stupid. I'm going to pitch here too." Misery loves company, it's true, and nearly frozen loves it more. We kept in touch through our tent walls in between naps for the next few hours.

The weather broke around dinner time. We both crawled out in our soaking clothes and walked into a patch of sunlight. Then we hopped around excitedly and threw our hands into the air saying "We lived! We're going to make it!"

When we got to highway 28 the next day, we thumbed down a semi-truck. The driver talked about his schedule and how the vehicle operated. Their lives are nuts, but so were ours. We seemed to have a nice understanding.

I had a three-pound bag of homemade cookies to get me through the 170 miles. My longest carry on this trail. Six days. And thanks to my amazing friends, Jocelyn and Mary, for supplying the edible joy.

Stabby, Banjo, and I go our separate ways tomorrow. We're celebrating with root beer floats in Lander, Wyoming. We are back to where we first flipped. Now it's time to flop. I'm going northbound from the New Mexico border. They are heading south from Steamboat.

Fingers crossed for a less than three-day hitch for my 575-mile journey to Chama.

Knowing that I was back on my own, I felt grounded. Having no answer to the question of how I would be crossing the land between my feet and Chama, I felt empowered. I walked through Lander toward the highway to celebrate the spirit of adventure and to see what it had to teach me.

That's when the magic happened.

Perhaps you can recall a kind of person in your life who's easy to treat. One who likes what they like loudly. Walk down any city block with them and you'll have three ideas before the crosswalk. I used to feel less than cool when people described me that way, like it was lame to be in love with everything all the time. Now, I am relentlessly grateful for it.

Climbing into the passenger seat of an SUV on a July day changed my life. For it was the first time I paid full attention to what happens when two generous souls share a journey. We saw a friend and picked up where we left off. Never mind the fact that we were strangers.

His name was Dan Abernathy. He's a large man physically, for the sake of definition, but more so, by spirit. With his loose flowing pants and long gray hair sticking out of a straw hat, I felt welcomed by the sight of him. Or was it something his eyes were putting out? It doesn't really matter. As soon as I climbed in, we were partners on a journey.

He belly-laughed at my admitted insecurity. "People in my life have careers and business plans. They have goals and clubs and 401ks. And me... I'm just walking." He loved it. I'll make that decision ten times more on the wings of how truly glad he was for who I am and how I shared it. It's an honor to be seen.

He told me about his heartbreak. Losing his baby sister to cancer. We cried together for our sisters and their suffering. He inspired me to write and gave me a signed copy of one of his poetry books, I Don't Shave on Sundays. Then wished me luck and drove off. I looked around at the ground I stood on, feeling carried.

I continued to be carried. Cracked open now, I stuck out my thumb. Beautiful people helped me cross that distance, one right after another. When I jumped out of a man named Warren's vehicle in Chama, New Mexico, the next evening, it was as though I had landed softly in a gas station parking lot by a gently rolling tidal wave. I've never felt so inspired. Eleven times climbing into the passenger door. Eleven strangers handing me off, sharing their stories, and opening their hearts. As soon as I checked into my hotel room, I wrote this:

Hitch

July 23, 2015

Go and Cry with a Stranger
Do it in their Car.
Get in their car, completely in.
Take your heart out and put it in their Teeth.
And Listen.

Listen to them say they work too much.

Listen to them say they're underpaid. Hear them geek out on how their truck works.

Let them crack you open a Bud, even if you think it's yucky.

Listen to them talk about the land they love, and the wife they lost.

The way they can't seem to find love, or make it stay.

Listen to the way death scares them.

Relate to them, admitting that as women in our late 20s, we're turning into mothers, whether we want to admit it or not.

Let them tell you you're courageous.

Let them lecture you on how you're crazy.

Listen to them talk about how hard it is to control their teenager or run their business.

About how they'd kill for their mama.

About being there when the Berlin Wall came down.

About how they got in trouble and cleaned themselves up.

How your health is everything.

How family is everything.

How they lost their daughter and granddaughter in a plane crash in Alaska.

Listen to how they believe there is good in all of us, though it can be hard to see.

Listen to them speak of holding their baby sister in their arms as she slips away.

Talk about Cancer.

Talk about being someone's sibling.

Talk about being in the room with death

and how it was beautiful, and sad.

And Cry.

Tell them the Truth.

Tell them you're Scared too.

Show them you're Alive.

And then they'll walk with you...Always.

 Perhaps the most impactful ride was with Manuel, who picked me up somewhere outside of Salida, Colorado. He was on his way to the vet to pick up two kittens he had spayed.

Manuel walked with a limp, a veteran with tarnished skin and a posture that suggested pain. He clung to my attention but was in no way threatening. It seemed he desperately needed someone to listen to him.

Manuel spoke of his struggles with health care. Many things he needed but could not afford. He talked about failed relationships and fear of never finding love. He confessed to rage he was not proud of. It may seem strange to hear, under those circumstances, but I'm asking you to put down those expectations and imagine starting from trust. Imagine looking at the stranger in the driver's seat as yourself, without any particular territory for claiming.

Manuel needed compassion like medicine and I was glad to dispense it. I wonder how many times a stranger has looked at him and shrunk away from his desperation. I wonder how many hurt people I have done that to.

I wonder what it's going to take for our people to rise.

I began hiking north the next day with power propelling me more than I could ever understand. Love was with me.

The Fun State

August 4, 2015

Greetings from colorful Colorado. In the last week and a half, I've made it almost halfway through the state. Miles are flying by. I saw more hikers on my first 10 miles along the Colorado trail than I have all summer.

The San Juan Mountains are beautiful. In a 120-mile traverse, nearly every bit of it was a glorious walk above tree line. The views were vast and colorful, and for the first time during this hike, I was able to average 30 miles a day into Lake City.

There I found the first hostel I've come to on this trail. Right as I limped in to find a bunk, a familiar face popped out the front door. It was Spoonman, whom I spent a few days walking with on the PCT. I dropped my things instantly and gave him a bear hug. We caught up for the next night and stayed up around the campfire playing songs and howling at the moon.

Sara-Tide surprised me. She had a bit of time between jobs and offered road support. There's no one on this planet that I've walked with more and getting to share camp with her each night has been a gift. A giddiness overtakes me each evening when I know I'm getting close to the road she'll be waiting by.

We're in a 1.2 star hotel tonight. I've got my feet soaking, and I'm excited to get back out there. I've gone over 2,000 miles this summer. It's hard to tell since it's all out of order, and it hasn't been important to me to keep track. But the men I was hiking with knew some of those numbers. The end is drawing near.

I Came, I Saw, I Faceplanted (A Colorado Story)

August 24, 2015

Colorado is complete and it's been something else. I've never spent so much time above tree line. Memories of barreling down ridges to dodge the lightning will be in my heart and nervous system for always. The trail through Colorado is one long, spectacular path along the spine of the continent. The CDT continues to expose me, and it's taught me a lot. I'm thankful to be out there and wide open, fully aware of the dangers, but saying yes, just the same.

The Adventure Within the Adventure

August 31, 2015

I've been withholding a side story and it's time I let it loose.

One early July morning in West Yellowstone, I walked into a bike/ coffee shop (Freeheel and Wheel) to be a mooch. A grumpy one at that. I was trying to find a local to get a package to Old Faithful Inn for me, since the post probably wouldn't beat me there.

A handsome, smiley fellow, we call him Craig, was unannoyed and genuinely interested in my quest. He found me a friendly local to carry the package within minutes and we exchanged numbers after a quick date at the Taco Bus later that afternoon. We hit it off, but I didn't realize what an impression it had made on me until I walked out of town.

It changed the game. I was thinking about quitting up to that point, but something about the way he took interest in what I was doing reminded me why I was out there in the first place.

He mentioned he was running the Beaverhead 100k that following weekend. A race fresh on my mind, having just come through the area. Turns out he's a fellow Minnesota native. There were unique parallels between us, him in West Yellowstone and me in West Glacier, both loving the hell out of life and running around mostly solo.

I called him after Beaverhead to see how he did for the 100k (quite well). Before long I was calling him in every town. And within weeks of meeting him, I was running my tail off through Colorado to get to his first 100-mile race.

I hiked all of Colorado in three and a half weeks so that I could rent a car and pass through his neck of the woods a day before his race. His dad, a couple friends of his, and I were his crew last weekend. I ran the last stretch with him and could barely keep up. It didn't seem possible that this happy guy, rock hopping down steep terrain, had just run 90-some miles and was coming up on hour 28 with no sleep.

I spent two days with him after his race, during which he walked around like nothing had happened. Then he drove me up to Helena and sent me on my way. He's coming to Glacier next week for the big finish.

I'm hooked. He's been a great inspiration for me on this trail and I'm embracing this adventure with the same wide-open arms that I've had on this walk.

Sometimes We're On Fire

September 2, 2015

It's the home stretch. Two hours ago, I crossed into East Glacier, Montana. It was a three day walk to the town of Lincoln from Helena. I had the company of Tom, a hiker from Israel, which helped take my mind off my thirst. Thick smoke was everywhere. And water sources were few. I carried four liters, twice what I usually carry, and still it was one of the thirstiest days I've ever had.

When we got to the humble town of Lincoln and ate our weight in junk food, we got news from hikers ahead that the Bob Marshall Wilderness was closed. That meant a 113-mile road walk from Augusta, MT into East Glacier. We hitched ahead to join a group of six others, including Stabby and Banjo. And thus began a different kind of adventure.

If you would have told me years ago that I was going to end up walking highway 89 for four days, I might have laughed at you. I at least would have raised my eyebrows and doubted the possibility. Yet, after a summer of walking the Continental Divide, nothing seems hard to believe.

Locals in small-town Montana have stopped to ask what the hell we are doing. A nice couple, Micah and Jo, hosted us in Choteau, which is no small feat, considering there are eight of us.

I didn't anticipate how touching it would be to come to Glacier with the view from the plains. Just like the first time I saw it 14 years ago, when it changed my life forever. Here I am today, more in love than before.

If you ever want to love your home more, I recommend spending a whole summer journeying toward it. I'm here now. The fires are subsiding, and the trail re-opened today.

Worth It

September 8, 2015

Worth it?

How can I even talk about this?

Worth the time? The steps? The discomfort? I guess I'm not sure what you mean.

Yesterday I stood waist deep in Grinnell Lake. Fully clothed in the icy rain. I ran into it and yipped like a coyote. I did it because I couldn't help it.

It's worth it to me to spend days in the elements. For the gratitude it gives me. I want to get rocked—that's what I'm after.

It's worth it to me to design my life around these adventures. It's worth every penny I earn. And then some.

Oh, the things which are worth it to me.

Exposure. As internal as it is external. From the inside out.

If I didn't stand like I do, if I didn't put it all out there, if I didn't grin at the clouds that roll in, I'd be someone else.

So, "worth it" is not a question that makes sense.

I don't make sense.

How I'm able to stand here, with my feet firmly planted on the ground and my head in the clouds, is something I've given up trying to understand. I suppose that puts my heart everywhere. Which is just right.

Boundary

September 12, 2015

The last few days happened the way they should. Love walked with me, in the form of Craig, and of everyone. Being reunited with Glacier is like being water in a river that finally made it to the widespread ocean. Now I get to float and expand.

It snowed on the first day. Enough to make me wonder if we were going to be alright. Craig was a trooper, high-spirited and tolerant. I thought it was appropriate that he got to see what this trail holds. Which is an edge. A place where you wonder. A place where it's up to you to make decisions and find a balance of not underestimating them while not losing your faith in yourself. A place where I never dreamed I'd spend so much time alone. Now I wonder when I can return.

After a shivery evening walk, we pitched our tent and made dinner. It was warm in the cold. Warm because of him, warm because of how I've learned to survive, warm because it always is. I may seem over-charmed, but I can't help it. I look around at all of us when we're shivering, and I think about how lucky we are to feel.

The next day we ate lunch by the shore of Waterton Lake. My body was hesitating to move past that point. The last four miles of Glacier were the biggest thing on my mind. Up to this point, I hiked every mile of trail in the park, barring the last four of the CDT. A perfectly ridiculous thing to do. Me, in a nutshell. Combining Glacier completion with it being the end of the trail this summer, which felt more like the end of three trails, which felt more like the focus of my life for the last five years, it was too much. I didn't know how to handle it. I still don't.

We stashed our stuff at Goat Haunt and ran for it. Which was perfect. Don't think about it, just do it. There was the boundary trail junction first. Which meant my last step on new-to-me Glacier trail. I stopped to acknowledge it, thought about 14-year-old me, gazing at Bowman Lake and realizing that something had changed forever. I thought about 27-year-old me, sitting on that log last summer wondering what I would feel if I should be so lucky as to walk here from Mexico on some September day. I thought about the .9 miles to go. I'm surprised I didn't burst into flames.

We ran on, had a moment with a raging stream, and soon enough, there it was. The border. That ominous clearing in the trees. My stomach turned and shoulders tightened as I fought my body's lurch back. Like seeing a ghost. Then I sped into a sprint to the terminus.

My ears rang as I came to a halt. I looked around and tried to see with all of me. It was hard to make sense of anything. There I was. There *it* was. What was I supposed to be doing or feeling?

We sat next to each other with our backs against the spire, looking south. I searched the Cathedral Peaks across Waterton Lake for answers. *This?* I asked inside my head. *I feel nothing.*

I heard a gentle voice reply, "Yes." It looked as if the mountains were rolling with laughter.

I got mad for a second. Inside my head I snapped, *That's not an answer!* Before I understood why, I began laughing.

There was nothing waiting for me at the end of my long journey. Whatever accomplishment or approval I sought was within me the whole time.

I cried, then laughed again. Moments later, we got up and walked back.

That's the end, but I don't suppose I believe in endings anymore.

Te Araroa, NZ

2017/2018

3,000 Kilometers (1,864 Miles)

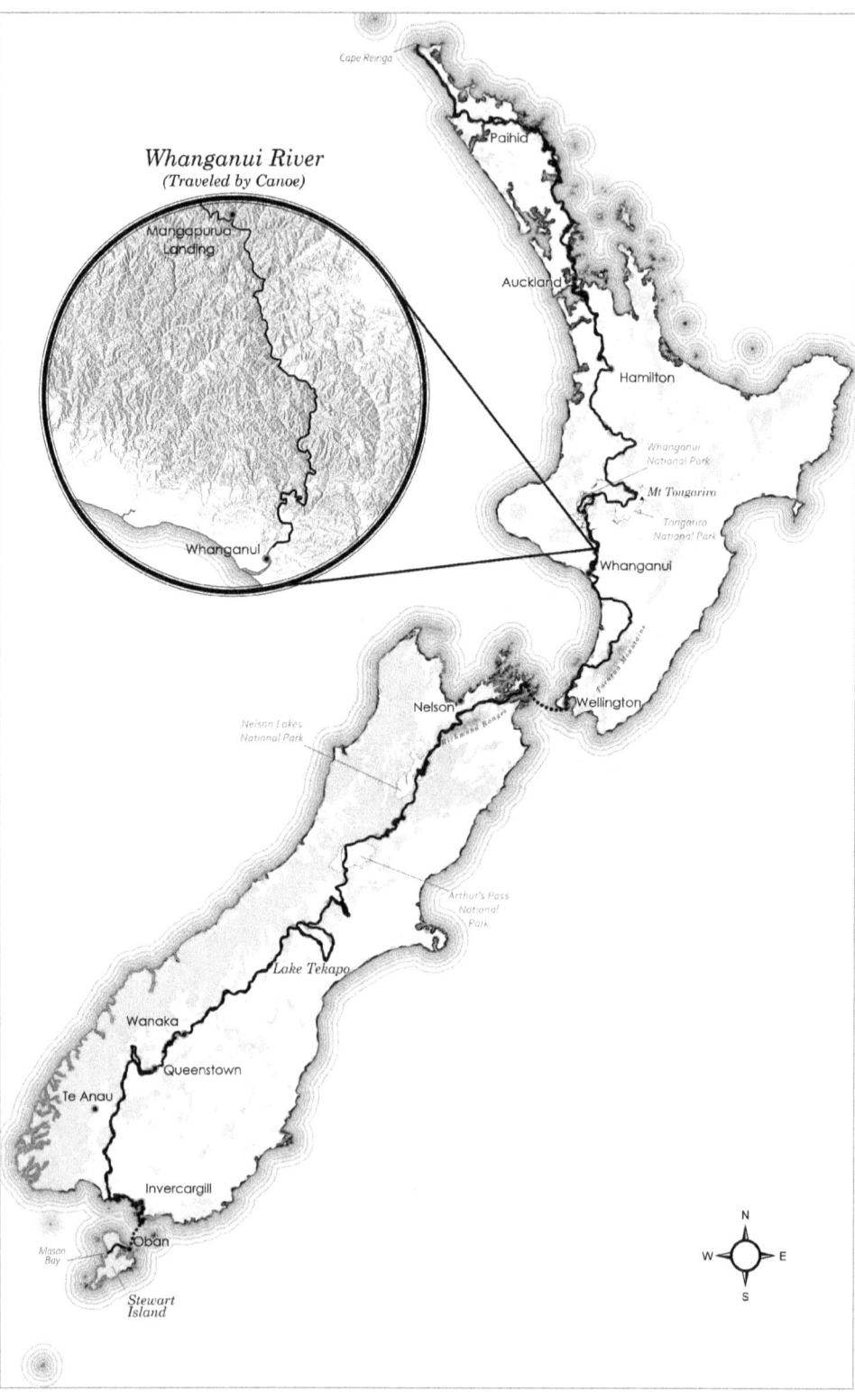

Whanganui River
(Traveled by Canoe)

Mangapurua
Landing

Whanganui

Cape Reinga

Paihia

Auckland

Hamilton

Whanganui
National Park

Mt Tongariro

Tongariro
National Park

Whanganui

Tararua Mountains

Nelson Lakes
National Park

Nelson

Marlborough Sounds

Wellington

Arthur's Pass
National Park

Lake Tekapo

Wanaka

Queenstown

Te Anau

Invercargill

Mason
Bay

Oban

Stewart
Island

N
W E
S

The things changing in my life in the next two years were obvious and yet unnamable. I came off the CDT carrying slight disturbance. Though my intrapersonal journey was beautiful, the environment was on my mind; the deep thirst I felt in the wildfires, the smell of cattle on the land, and the flux of tourism in places like Yellowstone. Visitors were running across ancient biomes to make videos or picking up baby bison to put in the trunk of their car.

It was in that time that I became a freak for not having a smart phone. It also became impossible to stay away from screens so long as you're near others. I kept a whiteboard at my waitressing job of how many days I could go without someone putting a video in my face. I never got past 1. I watched tourism turn into tables of families all on their tablets and people tripping over logs from walking with a recording screen held out in front of them. I was uncomfortable with the change in our culture. I wanted nothing more than dirt and fresh air and considered screens to be their antithesis.

After the CDT, I was craving connection vehemently. And pretty sure we were all going up in flames.

What led me to that conclusion? Well, flames.

On August 10th, 2017, the unthinkable happened. The Sperry Forest, my spiritual birthplace, caught fire in an evening thunderstorm. I joked earlier that day with the Sperry Chalet employees that it seemed like a safe patch of Glacier. Fires were springing up everywhere, but the cedars, larches, cottonwoods, and western hemlocks of that pocket of paradise were a rainforest. A high divide to their west trapped 10 inches more annual rainfall than surrounding microclimates, as well as ash from the eruption of Mt. Mazama 7,700 years ago. The hydrophilic forest floor could be mistaken for the pacific northwest with its moss-covered rocks and numerous ferns. And some of those trees were over 700 years old and as wide as a car.

When I heard that lightning had struck near Crystal Ford (four miles from Sperry Chalet), I found it impossible not to take personally. Just as I had the election of 2016. As well as the fact that my beloved aunt Lu was in her final months with us, due to ovarian cancer.

After the lodge at Sperry Chalet burned down, I hiked around Lake

MacDonald. I watched the fire from the shore with my head tilted 3,500 ft above the lake and my back resting against a fallen log from the Robert Fire in 2003. With a deep breath for every cloud of black plumage that rose into the sky, I said goodbye. I was going to the Midwest to support my aunt for her final days. And after that, New Zealand. Maybe forever.

About

November 21, 2017

In a couple short weeks, we begin our journey across New Zealand. It's a 3,000 km hike across the entire country, starting at the northern point of the North Island, continuing all the way to the southern point of the South Island.

This will be a different animal.

Firstly, it's a thru-*tramp*. A new culture. That's sounding pretty good these days.

It's also new terrain; jungle-like forests and estuaries. We will be spending the first month or two in wetness. Notes like: "dry off here" or "hang up your wet socks at this place" appear often in the guidebooks. Rain will be a big portion of the water we encounter, but there's also swampland, ocean beach walks, and several incomplete parts of trail where the only option to connect the dots is by waterway. One of those points, in fact, is over 100 km on the Whanganui River.

With this water comes a new set of awareness. We will need to study tide tables and weather forecasts to be on the lookout for flash floods in river canyons.

And we're a *we*. Craig and I will be hiking together, his first thru-hike and my first duo. It will be interesting to see how I compose myself with a witness.

More than ever, I feel like I am returning to myself. I feel like I've been out of place for the last couple of years. I need the trees.

I appreciate all of you who've followed along with my previous walks. I hope to share this one with you. Hope it's a good one, full of peaks and valleys, tears and honor, depth and transformation. I hope to come out closer to the ground. Closer to my fellow human. With light.

Kia ora!

Calling Yesterday

December 9, 2017

Our journey to New Zealand didn't ask much of us. We laid over in Hawaii, breaking the commute with a day on the beach. Craig and I felt light-hearted once we were airborne, after painful good-byes, worries about the things we might have forgotten, and aches for the things we will miss.

The gravity of leaving my county for a year has carried a heaviness for months leading up to today. A couple of the best women in my life will be having babies while I'm gone, two more will be getting married, and a person I can't imagine living without will be going on the greatest journey any of us will ever know. None of this comes without depth.

That's why I was surprised to find that coming to a place like New Zealand does feel easy. Seeing its beauty, knowing it's a place full of travel networks and smiling faces. Organic farms and sauvignon blanc. Of peace.

That's it. My heart knew it right away. Peace. In the bright blue waters rolling across the sand. In the fern-covered forest. In the eyes of a man selling me coffee.

May we always feel small.

May we always feel lucky.

May we always be connected.

We're getting settled in Auckland this weekend. We got a phone and missing pieces of gear and supplies for the journey. We enjoyed good meals, expensive beer, and a swing dance lesson in the park. For my first phone call from New Zealand, as well as my last from my US phone, I called Lu. She was still living out Friday while I was living Saturday. I flew to tomorrow. How lovely to find that what it holds for us is sunshine, adventure, and a place where we can trust each other.

I walk with my family. I walk with my dearest friends. I send my love on the wings of the wind and I speak to you through the trees. I hope there is peace in your hearts, and I know no way to be closer to you than here on the ground.

Peace be the Journey. Long May we Walk. For the Love, ALWAYS.

Tomorrow, We Hike

December 11, 2017

After getting our ducks in rows (or something kind of like them) in Aukland, we were whisked out of the city by a native. Her name is Raquelle Devine and I met her at a trailhead in Glacier a few years ago. It was a winter morning, and I thought I was there alone until the sliding door of an unassuming van swung open to reveal a smiling traveler. She ended up coming to my going away party that night and stayed in my cabin with me as I prepared to step out for my CDT hike.

Since then, she's been offering to receive us and set us on our hiking track. She took us to her home a couple hours north and introduced us to the plants and birds. "Hungi hungi," she plucked a dark green, glossy leaf from beside an ocean trail, "eat it."

We were approaching a wildlife sanctuary with rare birds, including the Takahe, which were nearly driven to extinction and down to 300 living. She told us some of the conservation strategies of New Zealand to protect the ground birds from predators like weasels and possums. The largest conservation effort in the world, I've been told.

The forest here is like nothing I've ever seen. It's lush and Jurassic, made extra dramatic by rocky shores and crashing waves behind it.

My appreciation for the ocean has caught me off guard. I thought I knew water, but this is different. Deeper.

Raquelle is putting together a non-profit organization to help monitor and remove plastic in the ocean. A true warrior for a cause. It's refreshing to talk openly about the things that are impacting our planet and how much action is being called for.

I was happy to shift to the metric system. Getting to know kilometers and celsius felt adaptive and present. New Zealand acknowledged both systems, which was representative of its people and philosophy. After all, it was a country with a 37-year-old woman for its Prime Minister and a national anthem sung in both English and the native tribal language, Māori.

90-Mile Beach

December 20, 2017

We began our hike at 6:30 pm on Tuesday, December 12th, on the northern most point of New Zealand, Cape Reinga. The Māori honor this as a sacred place where spirits make their transition to the afterlife. The waves crashed together and formed a seam of ripples as far as the eye could see. It's here that the Tasman Sea meets the Pacific Ocean. I heard the crash of the waves for kilometers, a mighty thump that suggests profound power. The ocean has the same effect on me as the night sky, half mesmerizing, half intimidating, all magical.

We ended up meeting new plants with our shins, offering our skin in a bushwack for the first hour of walking. All to stay inland during high tide. We didn't make it far before the sun started to set. Spreading our camping pads, we watched our first ocean sunset and were soon introduced to the frontrunners of the southern stars.

I watched them appear like a movie fan next to a red carpet, with giddiness and anticipation. The first thing I noticed was Orion upside-down, or is it right-side-up? What a great new perspective. This was the overlap my family could see from their own night view. The rest of the sky was new. I felt my ten-year-old self in my heart, learning the constellations in quiet wonder.

Later that night, I had my first glimpse of the southern cross. A sense of arrival washed over me with the crashing waves.

Our lips blistered from sun exposure, but we got the hang of it after the second day. Cover everything. Duh! We timidly attempted to swim in the ocean, laughing at the waves and the pull of the sand under our feet, squealing and jumping back from the jellyfish floating between our legs.

Our third night we came to a hostel/forest restoration area known us Utea. There were kittens and delicious smoothies provided by vibrant and friendly hosts.

They told us that the jellies are harmless. All of New Zealand is. That news provided the missing piece for a much better swim. That evening we jumped waves and rode them to shore. How is it that I have spent so little of my life thinking about the ocean? The world is 71% water. I can't forget it now.

The next day we made it to a beach town called Ahipara. In the last few kilometers of walking I had reception for a great talk with Lark (Aunt Lu and Uncle Mark). It was more than great, one of my favorites, though I've had a lifetime full of them. Lu believes in me and always makes it clear. I'm counting my tremendous blessings on this walk.

The Kauri

December 21, 2017

There's a beauty of a tree that grows up to 50 meters tall. They have trunks up to 16 meters in circumference and live for over 2,000 years. It's not something to see, it's something to behold. And its name is Kauri.

New Zealand possesses the most stunning forests I've seen so far. We're surrounded by layers of thick greenery: ferns, moss, mud, webs of roots, tunnels of vines, and that's only what we perceive by sight.

We're in Pahia now. A beach town bumbling with water activity. Dan Dan the Kayak Man took our packs yesterday in Kerikeri so that we could trail run for the last two hours. He overheard us talking at the hardware store and offered. It didn't feel weird to hand our whole lives over to him. Helping strangers to this level is a common practice. A given, like holding a door open for one with arms full.

Today we're in paradise, spending our first day off lying on the beach. Tomorrow, we kayak the trail with friends.

It's not all rainbows and sunshine. The trail has been a proper challenge, with steep traverses and lots of slippery mud. I've fallen on my face at least three times, likely more. Yet, there is something about the forest. Even though it's relentless to hike it's got a way of energizing us. We've gone 247 kilometers. That's almost 10%. Gone too fast, I'd say. What a trail.

Rough Water

January 3, 2018

I think one of the better parts of hiking a long trail is the suffering. Maybe not the actual suffering, but certainly the moments of glorious turmoil where you think you've met your end. This is a story about Craig, me, and the fin above water between us.

We were resting into the ease of this journey, reflecting on kind strangers who've helped us and the luck of our timing for tide crossings. Two days before, we walked a 44-kilometer day where our first steps were an estuary crossing perfectly timed at low tide, then twelve and a half hours later we were taking our final steps in the same low water, at a different estuary.

On New Year's Day, while expressing our gratitude for hummus wraps, we looked down at our map as our smiles quickly sank into the sand. *WARNING: DO NOT CROSS AT HIGH TIDE.* Where we were sitting, we were four kilometers from it and an hour past low tide. We jumped to our feet and ran for it.

Then came the rain.

I don't ever oppose rain. There are times that my soggy feet make me a bit grumpy, but I always recognize rain as good. I want the trees to have it. I want the grass to stay green. There are few things in life I dread more than going thirsty, and I try to understand how the plants must feel in a drought. So, rain yes, but then estuary crossing, not so much.

The water looked flooded at first glance. Craig and I were several meters apart, trying to negotiate our own path across the mud, when he started crossing the river behind me.

"I don't know that it's safe." My yell was barely audible over the plunking water.

"I just want to see how it goes." He said.

I followed with hesitation. The water was murky and moving steadily. Nothing about it felt right.

Craig was in the low thigh range, and I, closer to shore, was at knee level when I saw a pointed appendage skim the roaring surface. It could have been an illusion, perhaps the ripple of the waves from the rapids. A dark shadow underneath the ripples disqualified my denial. I stood frozen and tried to stay calm.

"Craig, there's something in the water." It flashed again, as I spoke.

Craig saw it between him and I. His eyes widened and he let out a yell as he barreled full speed toward the opposite shore. It got deep quickly. I watched helplessly as the milky brown water reached his chest. He fluttered around in circles, backpack and all, with a similar anxiety to a dog that can't find its ball.

For what felt like several moments he flailed around, then resolved to make his way back toward me. My whole body clenched until he managed to plop into the sand beside me.

We sat breathless on the shore for a few minutes, taking inventory. Things were wet that we needed dry, and we had a long way to go around. It was a different set of facts to sit with than those of our hummus retreat the hour before.

The ocean won't let you get the impression that you control things. Which is the beauty of adventure. You don't. Step lightly and hope for the best.

And maybe pay more attention to tide tables.

Two hours later, during the walk around the river, we happened by a lovely bridge across the estuary that had just kicked us around. As we watched the water, the same fin appeared. "There it is," Craig sped up to the highest point of the bridge to look down.

From the high vantage point, we saw the animal underneath it. It was wide and flat. The supposed shark fin was actually the wing of a stingray. We laughed, we marveled, and we kept walking.

Friendly As

January 3, 2018

We've been hiking from home to home, through a network of people who make themselves known to hikers. They share their beautiful dwellings, feed us fresh produce out of their gardens, include us in family barbeques on the beach, and participate in campfire song circles.

And then there was Tidesong, where our hosts invited us to sit at their table for dessert after family Christmas. Hugh and Ross were hikers and bikers themselves with a lot of understanding and insight. They live at an estuary crossing and offer guidance for timing and direction. From the dock of their property the whole family stood waving as we stepped on. They nodded reassurance when our feet disappeared into the sucking mud. We all laughed as we plucked our feet from the seafloor with playful gratitude, which paired nicely with the pocket full of pancakes they gave us upon departure.

We rang in the new year with new friends. A kiwi family found us walking a highway in the afternoon and insisted that we spend the night in their cabin. Margi and Rob work hard to keep New Zealand strong and well. Rob is a social worker specializing in teenagers and Margi is an elected city board member who, among many things, has headed up a project to put in a bike route for Auckland's commuters. We stayed up till midnight with them and their teenage daughter, Tess.

In this most populated part of the country, it's practically a sandwich-to-sandwich hike. A concept I very much enjoy but truly don't feel that I've earned. We've been walking for three weeks and haven't made a dent in our tummy rolls. We haven't been too hungry, or achy, or dirty in this land of no strangers.

Hey Farmer Farmer

January 17, 2018

The hardest surfaces to walk are the farm tracks. They are hot, steep, choppy, covered in poo, overgrown with thorns, thistles, and gorse (which I would describe as stinging nettles' bigger and meaner cousin). When we come to farm tracks, which usually begin with a few big hoists over stiles that guide you over barbed wire, I get whiny and protest, hoping it can change the course of my next couple hours. Alas, it doesn't. Turns out the universe doesn't rearrange for you when you don't feel like going through something.

The other day we were walking out of the Waitomo Caves area, leaving a visitor center. I had reception and called my mom. There would be road walking for a bit and perhaps we would be in reception for a while. We were speaking for about three minutes, when we came over a style into a vacant cow pasture. I apologized for being out of breath as I walked up the steep, grassy pitch. Grateful to talk to her and pleasantly surprised that my little sister was with her.

We hopped another stile into a field with cows. It's a common occurrence on the TA, but something didn't feel right. There was a bull in front of us stomping its hooves and projecting a warning wail. I laughed, grateful for my mom to witness some of the shenanigans of hiking. Craig flashed me a severe look. The bull was galloping toward us.

We ran to the next stile and jumped over it just in time. Then looked around for another way through the pasture. What we found were more bulls, with the same general attitude toward us. While trying to talk to my little sister about her new job, I had the revelation that I should get off the phone to free up both hands for fence hopping. She agreed.

We opted to road walk around the pastures. It would add a few kilometers, but it sounded like a great alternative.

In lighter farm news, we got to hike with an ostrich. Behind a fence, it walked beside us for several minutes, then waved goodbye and looked bummed out when we walked beyond its parameters. Who knew they made such pleasant walking mates?

Thanks Mom and Mackenzie, for putting up with me.

Glimmer

January 31, 2018

For many kilometers after Auckland, the Te Araroa's route takes you road walking. Not the fun kind either. You walk by the airport, large warehouses, water treatment plants, shopping malls, expensive hotels, and are at times crammed into a narrow shoulder of a major highway. Add rainstorms to the mix, and you've likely got yourself a grumpy pants.

On the second day of soggy road walking, a man pulled up beside us in his truck. "Hey, TA hikers. I bet you'd appreciate a place to stay indoors tonight."

We responded wide-eyed with some drooling and head nods. He wrote down his address and said we would be there in a couple hours' walk, which he knew from hiking the trail last year.

We skipped along the road after that and despite a steep climb through mud and thistles, found ourselves at his doorstep still smiling. He fed us, gave us beer, and looked through the maps to give us pointers on trails ahead.

We set off the next morning to less rain, but more roads. We felt better for our nice stay indoors, but then came mud, heat, cows, and long, flat road walks. For days.

The stretch from Auckland to Waitomo, which is 300 kilometers, is at least 60% road walking.

That's why we were so amazed when we found the Pirongia Forest. Suddenly there were great views, well maintained trails, strikingly beautiful moss-covered trees.

After that forest, we were back to the road. A gravel one with little traffic. We found a spot to pitch that looked like an old mining road and drifted quickly into sleep. I woke up hours later to a rustling in the tree limbs above us.

The red glowing eyes of a possum stared down at me. We hadn't bothered with the rain fly that night and enjoyed watching the stars, but now we cringed watching the possum climb the tree limb six feet over our faces. I turned on my side, hoping if I slept through it, it would go away, then I gasped at something astonishing.

The stars were in the trees beside us. How could that be? I was certain a rock wall was there when I went to sleep. Then I realized what I was looking at. Glow worms. The starry night sky was sprinkled all around us. I smiled.

Road walks and possums aside, this is a wonderful place.

Naked and Nervous

February 1, 2018

We know there are varying degrees of what's appropriate for naked behavior from region to region. Most hikers/mountain folk that I know in Montana see it as a right. When you're in the trees, no one can get on your case for letting your butt cheeks shine. Especially when swimming in the cool mountain water.

In the Midwest, where I grew up, I have family members that can't handle us mentioning the naked bike rides in Portland and Seattle or our love for skinny dipping. When I was new to the mountain culture, I felt bold to swim nude. My surrounding company didn't think anything of it. It was normal.

We've been trying to navigate this situation in New Zealand. We are by water often. It's hard to get away from the ocean in New Zealand (not that we would want to). We usually dip in with our hiking shorts and, in my case, a sports bra. When we find ourselves alone on the coastline, we strip nude and run into the water with a sense of freedom.

The Te Araroa routes you down the Whanganui Journey. A three-to-five day float along an incredible river that sweeps through a wild and stunning canyon.

We were soaking up shade for a long lunch break just beyond the national park boundary. Not a boat went by for our hour-long lunch break of extravagant luxuries like jars of olives and cans of beer.

It was sticky hot. Our dip in the river was much anticipated and naturally, it was naked now that we were past the busy section. We dove in and came up smiling.

An unexpected sound rang over the valley. I chuckled and said, "That sounds like children." Mostly kidding, imagining a scenario one would find in some Ben Stiller film. The next moment, three kids in life jackets came running down the hill, heading right for the swimming hole we were nervously treading.

When I first got into the water, I was a bit of a snob about its color. "Montana streams are crystal clear" I said with longing as I put a foot into the murky unknown. Now the tinted shield was my ally.

The kids jumped in. Their dad came around the corner with an older boy, who swam laps across the river for training. Even in our time of awkwardness, we acknowledged that this boy was impressive. Craig and I had been timid about going two meters away from shore, let alone swimming across the current.

His dad watched and yelled coaching advice, all the while having conversations with us about our journey. He told us stories of growing up on the river. He was Māori and had many cultural ties to it. There were annual paddle trips, swimming lessons with uncles tossing you out of the boat, and sad stories of friends losing their lives. We had a surprisingly good conversation for floating heads with things to hide.

I was just about to brave up and ask him to toss me my swimming clothes, when he headed quickly toward his son and started yelling urgent directions to him, "Go with the flow! WITH THE FLOW!" The boy was in control but working hard.

The three kids jumping off the rocks behind us seemed distracted enough. I made a dash for it, 20 steps from concealment to clothing. I snatched them up, slipped them on, and tossed Craig his shorts. If the kids behind me noticed, they didn't let on.

As for the dad, he didn't turn around while I was out of the water, but I'm sure he knew the whole time. You don't grow up on the river without being able to recognize when you've caught someone with their knickers down.

Family

February 1, 2018

Strangers can be family. It happens when you travel. It happens all the time. It happens an awful lot in New Zealand.

I'm writing this at the kitchen table of the Wright family. They're at work. Livi and Gareth are teaching, and Riley is starting secondary school today. Their youngest son, Nixon, starts school next week and is with his grandparents. We get to stay within these walls and experience these moments with them. They gave us a key to their house when we first arrived, two days ago. They gave us their trust and we cooked them lasagna.

How did we get here?

Honestly, it didn't take much. About a week and a half ago, we celebrated my 31st birthday with a proper mountain beating. A day of crazy mud and cutty grass, which gave us thin lashes in every direction across our shins.

The next day was one we'd been rather excited for, the famous Tongariro Crossing. It's famous for being the place where Frodo destroys the ring, but its presence transcends the epic tale. Nary a volcano I've heard of can offer this much mystery and humility in a 20 kilometer jaunt.

We began our ascent in a storm. A thumping good one. We were socked into thick clouds with heavy rain and rampant wind. I took a few photos of my windblown, puffed out pants and the clouds all around us.

We didn't get much visibility, but there's always more. We could taste the sulfur. We could feel the winds of "Mt. Doom" telling us we were puny. We got wet.

As we approached the Mangatepopo hut, I tried to prepare Craig not to get attached to having room in the shelter. More than once on the Appalachian Trail, I can recall approaching shelters in the rain with relief on my mind only to catch squinty-eyed glares from people huddled underneath its awning. They don't make room for you. Or speak. Or move. Leaving you with no choice but to turn around and try not to cry.

We found the opposite. I'm pretty sure a Kiwi (New Zealand resident; not to be confused with the flightless bird or the fruit) would let you sit on their lap before expecting you to stay out in the rain.

We shared a table with a family, laughing and playing cards. There were two boys with their parents. Craig and I brewed coffee with tangible glee that made them laugh more. That's my deepest joy, the simple pleasure of holding a cup of something warm in my hand with insatiable gratitude. To have good people see us in that moment, in its bare bone honestly, took it a step deeper.

We chatted about adventure for a while and were soon invited to stay in their home. We had three days of walking and four days rowing before we would be to their charming town, Whanganui.

They scooped us up as soon as we contacted them and took us first to a marvelous rocky pier at dusk. The moonlight was shining brightly off the water, and the waves were crashing all around us.

It's so easy to love.

This timing is good for my soul. I'm beginning to cope with the reality of losing family in this house. I said my last, "I love you" on the phone yesterday. I went right to the piano and cried in minor chords.

I feel safer here, with the ocean to talk to, and a families' love to fill the space between the walls.

A special thanks to the Wright Family.

To the Ocean. To E Minor.

And to Lu. Always

The Tararua Range

February 6, 2018

After three days of road walking, including 20 kilometers on a busy highway, came something completely different. The Tararuas. A challenge that caught me off guard.

Somewhere amongst the roots and rocks we scrambled, was a trail worthy of respect as grand as the White Mountains in New Hampshire. I haven't been so properly thrown off my expectations since my Appalachian hike in 2011. From an average of 35 kilometers a day, we went into these woods thinking we could maybe slow it down to 25-30 for elevation. We collapsed into blobs of tired bones after 19.

On the AT, I was mad that I couldn't go faster. I would push along out of spite, thinking of the trail as my rival. As though it was something to defeat or outsmart. It's different now.

I've come to understand my stepping. I can generally do what I think I can do, making room for a few unexpected setbacks and incorporating sluff time. In this mountain range, my estimation was wrong. There's a hilarity to finding what you think you know to be way off. I eat my words, gladly.

I enjoy laughing at my expectations, for no matter how useless I know they are, they stay with me. Maybe there is a way to live with them, ac-knowledge their presence, and tell them to get lost all at the same time. Maybe it's good for me to really embrace what is not graceful about me. I can learn to be okay with all the parts of being human.

We can be greedy at times, maybe that helps us to really shine when we share. We are anxious, maybe that helps us to be extra beautiful when we open our hearts. We're all doing the best we can with what we've got.

I owe the mountains a thank you. Thanks for kicking me around and reminding me to loosen those expectations. It only took a moment or two to accept that I was going to be in those mountains for longer than I'd planned. A moment later, I knew I was lucky for it. An extra day was a gift.

Now, we are looking at a stretch known for being just as tough and twice the length. It's probably going to suck wonderfully.

Crossing Over

February 14, 2018

A small victory comes from completing the North Island. Craig and I were happy to do it as a bit of a run. It was 12 kilometers from our hostel to the southern shore, and we did it early in the salty morning air. I got a sense of everything being vivid like I was dreaming rather than perceiv-ing it; lighter on my feet and yet closer to the ground.

It was a beautiful run up and over some of Wellington's city parks. Among tall pine trees and sea views we gazed in all directions. The end of the track comes down to a rocky shore, jagged and ominous. Like a different sea than we've seen. Everything was mystic and alive.

Which was fitting, as it came with a phone call that changed my heart. In the first few minutes of our run my phone rang with the news I'd been anticipating; an inevitable truth I've been trying to get used to this whole hike. Lu, my beloved aunt, had passed.

It wasn't shocking. It wasn't particularly hurtful either. My body seemed to take over and run. To think little and breathe deeply and feel what's around me in hopes that it was a way to dedicate my senses among the living to the dead. Particularly the newly dead.

When we got to the southern shore we sat for a moment at the marker and acknowledged our journey. I jumped into the sea and thought about Lu's comments on my strange love for cold water. More than ever, I wanted to feel the sensations. I hoped I could share them with her.

For the rest of the day, being alive was my focus. I tasted my wine. I breathed in the ocean air. I felt the breeze on my skin.

We took a ferry to the South Island. It was our day to crossover, in a smaller way. Part of me grieved at the disappearing shoreline of the north island, feeling as though I was leaving her there. A bigger part of me knew I took her with me.

Next to the shimmering ocean I felt comforted. There is sadness, but it's nestled in beauty as my heightened senses take it in. Everything is part of it.

When the sun set that night, I grieved for the day to be ending. A day that had started with her in this world. I felt grateful, and deep. I had a cup of coffee, which is strange for me at night. I had to feel its warmth in my hand, its steam on my face, and to see it on the table next to a hand of cards that Craig and I played in her honor.

It's going to happen in pieces. A matter of learning what's gone the next time I go to reach for it. On a shallow note, I look at the surface of the sea and I wonder what I'm supposed to be feeling. On a deeper note, I know my heart understands things that my brain can't.

And I walk.

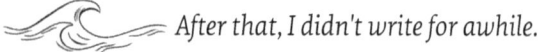 *After that, I didn't write for awhile.*

Things that Are

March 26, 2018

The magic finally hit me on a plateau before Lake Tekapo. We were eating our dinner on gradual mountain slopes, looking down at the lake framed in glaciated peaks. Somewhere between the satisfaction of having what you need and the grandeur of mountain valleys at dusk, I got that tingle down my spine. That breath spiraling inside my chest.

This. Exactly this. These are the moments I'm after. The gift of being at home in nature.

The trail never stops surprising us. We keep congratulating ourselves for getting through the big things to find there's another one coming. Things like dangerous (allegedly) river-crossings, which would be a 150 kilometer hitch-hike around if you can't pass through.

Quite often this trail is mapped to the edge of a waterway: lake, river, straight, estuary, what have you, and the kilometers stop counting on the north side and resume on the south. As if the space between doesn't exist. We are faced with the reality of how different things are in life than on paper.

It's good for us. We take the trail one section at a time. Carrying only the maps to our next substantial town stop. I feel knocked off my cloud when other hikers tell us what's ahead. Like they're spoiling the plot. I enjoy problem solving, and I want to be on my toes. At this point in my life, I'd rather have reactions than plans.

People ask me all the time, "What do you want to get out of this?" I haven't come up with an answer. I feel a need to tell them to un-ask the question. *This* is just as much about everybody as it is about me. It's about being, not wanting. There isn't much room here for *getting* or *having*. Which is something I'm learning more and more when I walk with that concept we call "loss." It's about smelling as much as it is about seeing, maybe more, and most of all, it's about feeling. Still, I don't set out with something to gain in mind, I hope that it can be something to give. To be.

Me and the things that are.

Through All Kinds of Weather

April 4, 2018

It's autumn in the Southern Alps. The smell of mulch is present and crisp leaves are falling from the trees. I welcome the quieting of tourist towns, the squash, and of course, the snow.

You don't realize where you've put yourself until you're deep in it. Seeing a few inches of snow on the ground didn't faze us on our lunch break on the Breast Hill Track, between Twizel and Wanaka. We ate our lunch inside the hut with a new friend, Damien, and spoke lightheartedly about our plans to move on. He thought we were insane but didn't want to be left behind. From lounging with a cup of tea to returning his feet into wet socks, we marveled at Damien's quick shift and then enjoyed his company on the snowy four-wheel-drive track.

I knew there would be more snow up high, but figured it wouldn't be enough to get lost in. Plus, there was a hut on the other side of the pass.

The wind and wintry mix was a bit bombarding at first, but we were used to it in 10 minutes. Delving into a conversation, we forgot to be upset. It was fun to see Damien, an Australian, in the snow. The conditions were favorable in comparison to all the recent rain. We get less soggy in snowfall.

Life looks scarier from the view out your window than when you're actually out there.

The hut that night was quite crowded, but oh so warm. A little too warm, with the mustiness of wet-hiker-foot (similar, but altogether more disturbing than wet dog) filling the air.

When I lay my head down to rest that night I thought about the oncoming town, Wanaka, glad to be adding fuel to the anticipation of its luxuries. Knowing I would soon be shouting, "Hallelujah!" when hot water comes out of a wall.

The next morning, we woke up to sunshine on the snow. As we began our descent toward Lake Wanaka we heard a French hiker chuckle, "Maybe today I will go for a swim."

"From snow to swim in one morning," I laughed. In no time we were next to a shimmering lake, ordering burgers from a café. Might as well keep on walking, and maybe things will keep on changing.

Te Anau

April 10, 2018

It's marvelous to be at the gateway into Fiordlands National Park. The town is small and busy but feels like a place where kids are growing up.

Yesterday we hiked the Kepler Track. A Great Walk here in New Zealand. These are designated trails meant to attract the bulk of foreign tourism. They are highly coveted and there are nine altogether. The Te Araroa coincides with two of them, both on the North Island. The Tongariro Crossing ("Mt. Doom") and the Whanganui Journey, our three-day paddle adventure. These hikes are world famous for their beauty and accommodations. The huts are pricey, but great for families and allow backpackers not to carry tents.

There are all kinds of opinions about this system in New Zealand. Mine is that their Department of Conservation is genius. Due to the influx of these nine tracks, much of New Zealand's vast wildland is unpopulated.

The Kepler Track was majestic. We marveled at the vast Lake Te Anau, surrounded by dramatic peaks and waterfalls. I love New Zealand.

Our next adventure off trail is Stewart Island. When we finish the Te Araroa, we will be at the ferry terminal to this small island. What better way to celebrate the end of our journey than to partake in more journeying. It should only take three-to-five days to hike across Stewart Island where there is a likelihood of seeing a rare bird called a Kiwi, which has become a dream for us. I've only seen photos of their gum-drop bodies and squinty whiskered faces with a beak like a walking stick for the blind. We heard one in the night a few weeks ago. A sort of ring-ding-ding mixed with witch-cackle woke me up and left me wondering if I was still dreaming.

It's hard to believe, but we only have a week left of walking.

Changes

April 10, 2018

For the last six days, I've been kind of a shithead, emotional and irritable at the things I can't change. Like clear-cut hillsides, cold rain carried by wind, and icy wet sports bras on my bare chest in the morning.

Still, I laugh at myself. Knowing all too well that it doesn't matter nearly as much as it seems to in the moment. The sun will dry my pack before long. My feet will get me to safety. It won't storm forever, and the path will end.

We're back to the time of year when human beings do more of their living indoors. I appreciate the changes. Even when I'm stuck in them. Seasons teach me what to savor and what to avoid.

The walk from Te Anau has been a complete sampling of the Te Araroa's offerings. We've had tall grasses (Tussock) that you can't see your path through, pole to pole navigation on mountain tops made difficult in low clouds, swallow-your-leg mud, a few rounds of *keep-moving-or-die*, wind, rain, sleet, trenches to jump across, cow pies to try to avoid, giant trees to climb over, rivers to walk through—the whole gamut.

Making it more difficult on ourselves, we committed to doing it extra fast. We wanted to make it to a hotel on Colac Bay last night, which meant a couple of 45 kilometer days in those conditions.

It was worth it. Reading my book under a blanket last night with a cup of hot tea beside me, I recognized that I was living a dream.

My dreams are simpler these days. I dream of naps in the sunshine on summer afternoons, fresh picked vegetables, the laughter of my family, a warm cup of coffee in my hands, a walk through the trees for fun and not because I said I would...my guitar. I think all this adds up to explain that I'm ready for this quest to be over. Not because I grew to dislike it for what it is, but because it's changing.

That's life, and that's yes. I am ready.

From Cape to Bluff

April 13, 2018

At 6:30pm on Thursday, April 12th, we found ourselves at the southern terminus of the Te Araroa.

To the hour, we tied up a four-month journey and stood there to take it in, but it's always difficult. In all my trail completions the final terminus has felt like any place. In this case, we didn't get to gaze out into the ocean and fathom our achievement much at all. It was soon overtaken by two RVs full of tourists taking their photos with the sign. We stepped aside and laughed. I guess this spot is famous for being the start of New Zealand Highway One. It's interesting how the same things can have such different significance.

We popped open a bottle of champagne with another hiker and then hurriedly drank it to get our shivering bums inside. After signing a guest book at the local oyster house, we dispersed with the half a dozen other hikers who finished that day. Going separate directions after walking the same journey for months.

Craig and I stayed in town at the local lodge. We listened to the patter of rain on the roof while we enjoyed a victory dinner of Chinese takeaway.

It sounds a bit unresolved, because it sort of is. The real end of this journey will be at Mason Bay on Stewart Island. We still have walking to do.

Sunset

April 22, 2018

So here it is, at last. The end.

From this point looking on there is no mass of land again until Cape Horn, the tip of South America.

The sunset was brilliant and all around us. An orange glow painted our eyes and skin and even, it seemed, the air between us.

The end of the land was a poignant metaphor. Now we've walked New Zealand. Now we're something different than when we started. Together and separate.

Now I stand with loss.

It could be said that in the last couple of years I've lost a lot. Understanding loss has been difficult. For what would it be without gain? It couldn't exist. Who would I be to dwell when I have so much.

To say that I have lost would imply that I once had. I don't know about that. It was more that I got to be with Lu and Max and Sperry and this partnership with Craig. It was always a fortunate togetherness of a non-possessive nature. I suppose we had each other, but it was more that we saw and loved each other with our choices, day by day. I don't know if we ever *have* anything. I feel like it could be a dishonor to all of them not to feel lucky. I'm so grateful for these things. I can still hear them and smell them. I can see them when I close my eyes. They are parts of me.

The sunset was vivid and alive in its moment. Also, symbolic. May the Earth rest now, may my bones rest too. May it be the beginning of something else. May the expansive ocean hold its mystery and may the edge of me bow to the edge of it.

I come to Nelson now to celebrate grateful sadness. I know the ocean will understand.

I find that now, as I write this in a coffee shop, I can go back to that sunset when I close my eyes. That it, too, has become part of me.

Long may we walk.

Craig and I went our separate ways after the hike. He flew back to the States, and I got a job at a seaside café owned by a friend from high school. My sole focus was healing. Allowing the grieving process to unfold. Lu was like a parent. On the hike, I hadn't even begun to unpack what I was feeling. Instinctively I knew that I needed space to let it run its course. I needed peace and spirituality. New Zealand was the right place for it.

To Ashes

November 1, 2018

She exists in a container now. Although she sort of doesn't. That's what makes it all so interesting to navigate.

There are many feelings. I'm left wondering which one to choose.

There's sentimentality, the most presumed. Take a little part of it with me everywhere I go.

There's the reality slam. Holding the vessel and thinking about what it means. I knew it would come to this, but it would have been impossible to truly imagine.

There's all the stuff in between that got me here. Images which have been shut out purposely, in hopes of not losing sanity. It's not erasable and it's taken a lot to steer my brain away. Just try.

There's wondering how to treat it. Is it sacred or is it nothing? Is it both or neither? Do I touch it with my fingers or scoop it with a plastic spoon? Should I pray in some way? Do I know how?

What I'm really trying to ask is, *"Can I keep you?"*

I already know that I can't. Then again, what do I know? I see her boisterous nod. "I'll walk with you," she'd say. "Just toss me in the garden. Put me in a coffee mug."

She deserves to be flung joyfully. But I know she doesn't mind if I hold on, for now.

There's humor and lightheartedness, mixed with ache and gratitude. Desire to keep her alive the way that's left for me.

Here we sit, with ashes.

For much of my time in New Zealand I believed I was going to stay forever. Then it came time to sign the paperwork to extend my visa and an ache to be with my family came over me. I fit in in New Zealand, and I dreamed of settling down there. But, at the end of the day, I couldn't imagine my life without grizzly bears.

I made my way back to Montana. To the vast, untamed wilderness that had my heart.

To Travel

December 28, 2018

When you write travel journals you spend time sorting out the parts of it that you hope to share with the folks back home. It isn't always honest, though it's meant to be kind. I find myself in this strange space of translating myself backwards. For I am a critter that changes a lot, while I am, even more, a critter who stays much the same.

To travel has become a gift of forgetting that I'm traveling. Realizing my home is inside my head. So, when I sit down to write or listen to the trees, I feel like *here* is where I've always been.

To travel used to be to collect. Now I'm learning about my greed, or at least starting to. To travel is to experience. There is no photo for later, there is only now.

No longer is it to compare. New Zealand is not America, the Alps are not the Rockies. Why am I thinking about the phrases and prices of where I once was. I am here now.

To travel well is to notice. The calls of the birds. The changes in the night sky. The smells.

The people. The way friends meet up. The pet names parents use for their children. It's taking notice of how Grandma's face always lights up when her granddaughter walks in the room. Or how John at the pub is always grumpy about the foam on his porter. How same-siders sit close in restaurant booths and take in the view.

Space. Who keeps it and who doesn't.

Power. What that word even means. If anything.

Nature. Are we part of it, or aren't we? Are we trying to be less so? Is that the truth about us?

I hope we all can appreciate the misunderstandings. Like the time I realized I was mistaking the word fear for fair when listening to friends. Or the time I couldn't tell if we were talking about beer or a bear. Which for many would be a big difference, but for me, produces a similar smile. I hope we all can give ourselves a chance to laugh in our own faces. To realize that the soil that grew us has given us certain flavors. Which is just information. No need to call it right or wrong.

I tell you what, friends and family, I am bringing home some changes. I've learned a bit about quality, kindness, and slowing down. I'm learning to make less assumptions. Not to be in a hurry.

I find my recent weight gain to be lovely. For it came from a lot of good drinks with a lot of gorgeous people. It came from love. The love of bread and olives and the knowledge that I might not want to have unlimited access to those things too often. For the first time ever, I don't mind. I'm glad for that.

I've learned that Americans are hard on themselves.

That first hit me in a hut with three lovely Germans. They marveled at my need to drop joy out of it. As though every step was owed to some ever-present viewer. Other cultures don't see why we can't miss the road walks. We feel like if we miss any steps, then we haven't done it.

"According to whom?" One of them asked.

I had no answer. When the Germans are telling you that you could stand to ease up, it's time to examine yourself.

Spending time with these ideas, I feel free. It's no wonder it's taken me 31 years to be okay with a bit of belly fat.

I sit now, in an American coffee shop and say thank you to my travels. It's not an ending, but it's a chapter I hope to honor.

Part III

Revolution

"Of course it is happening inside your head, Harry, but why on earth should that mean that it is not real?"

-J.K. Rowling

Appalachian Trail 2021

2,191 Miles

(after 6,500 Miles of hike-guiding, climate change research, and joyful expeditions across Glacier and the Alps)

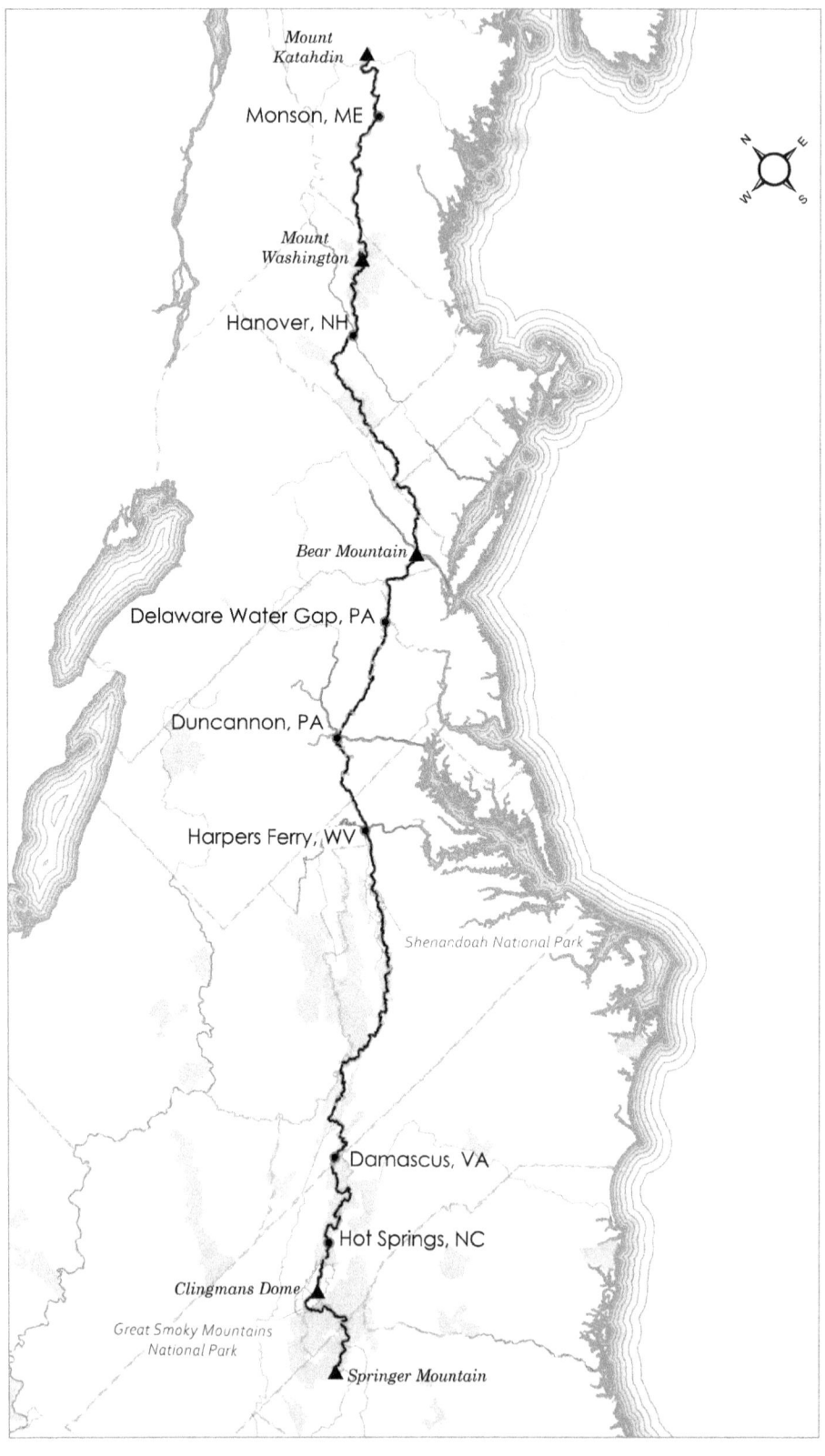

Mount
Katahdin

Monson, ME

Mount
Washington

Hanover, NH

Bear Mountain

Delaware Water Gap, PA

Duncannon, PA

Harpers Ferry, WV

Shenandoah National Park

Damascus, VA

Hot Springs, NC

Clingmans Dome

Great Smoky Mountains
National Park

Springer Mountain

Noticing

April 12, 2021

Last year at this time, I was watching the birds. Mostly from my porch with a dear friend and the Sibley Guide.

I was entranced. "Did you know American avocets put their wing around their mate while they walk side-by-side?"

"That's beautiful." He smiled.

"And blue-gray gnatcatchers build nests with spider webbing. To give it elasticity. So that as the chicks grow, the nest expands." I looked up from the book and beamed, "How cool is that?"

He had a satisfied look in his eyes, lovingly suggesting *I told you so.* He was a proud bird nerd for years and careful not to push it on me. There were times we'd hike together in Glacier where I would all but physically kick my foot into his behind after the fortieth time he got out his binoculars. My method of appreciating nature had always been in motion.

Eric and I were seasonal workers, accustomed to traveling during the spring and fall. A time of year referred to as mud season.

In times of COVID, rather than visiting my family in the Midwest or taking an epic road trip through desert rocks or Coastal Redwoods, I was watching the wonders from my front porch. Stalks of false Solomon's seal popped up and stretched their limbs. Clematis flowers opened as though they were crawling along vines with thin lavender arms. Chickadees were building a secret life together in the cavity of an expired birch tree. Watching them gather each little seed and twig was dinner entertainment. There was much to notice.

The family that I live with is especially inspiring. They appreciate nature. It's obvious in the things they've built, but even more so, in the two wild boys they've raised. They climb and run and crawl and ski and swim and paddle and do it all with contagious joy. The seven-year-old was giving me advice on what plants in our yard we could make into tea. The nine-year-old can skate-ski faster than me and identify sharp-shinned hawks and limestone before I can. I come to tremendous gratitude repeatedly for the allegiance we share heart to heart, and with the dirt we live on.

My dirt. That's an ache I've voiced often. It's an ongoing quest, "Until I find my dirt," I say, "I will be a rolling wheel. When I find it I will know, and I will care for it, and it will care for me. And it shall be my dirt." I still don't fully understand what I mean by that.

I am learning dirt from the ground up. It started between my toes, but I'm up to my fingertips now. When I plant seeds, my hands know the dirt and my lips say, "I honor and I thank you" as I pat the ground. I feel it in my chest when I say it.

Gardening was alive in me that spring. Jami and I put in hours and hours on our knees. The boys drove toy tractors through us and then got to work. Taking on challenges like Cottonwood roots; a worthy voyage for a boy with a pickaxe.

Our commitment to the garden was life-giving and not for the obvious. It was real and purposeful and un-messy in our brains. Growing food equaled *yes*. While so much of the pandemic and political climate left us unclear.

Eric and I went to numerous bird-watching hot spots. We squealed with delight when we saw our first American redstart. A pair of them were bouncing around a cluster of deciduous trees by the Swan River. Their big tails reminded me of the piwakawaka, or fantail, in New Zealand. A dear one. Their call sounds like a rusty wheel falling off a cart and they flick their tails around to catch gnats and mosquitos. One can appreciate their activity level, like a frantic spaz who lost their car keys. Reminding me all too much of myself.

We heard the squawk of a sora traipsing through the swamp. Though we never laid eyes on it, the sight of the tall grass bending to reveal its path was more than enough. I nearly caused a wreck on US 93 when I noticed the bright blue bill of a ruddy duck along the highway at Ninepipe National Wildlife Refuge. We even saw an American avocet, though it had no mate to put its arm around.

One morning in May, I did the thing I pressure myself to do most days, which was to lace up my running shoes while I'm still waking up. That way, fifteen minutes later, I find myself coming to in fascination, inspired by the morning light and the loud greenery around me. It worked, and after I experienced those sensations, I found myself gratefully returning to the gravel driveway. I glanced at the orchard, which was lush with life and color. I was accustomed to admiring the spring-green leaves and twisted gray bark over a blanket of yellow from numerous dandelions.

I stopped in my tracks. *The blanket is green. Where did the dandelions go?* They had been there the previous afternoon. I knew this well from an hour of yoga in the orchard shade. The grass was not freshly cut. *What the heck?* I stared puzzled then walked into the yard to investigate.

The dandelions were still there. They had closed. One or two of them were beginning to open. I felt like a child who had just caught her mother hiding Easter eggs in the yard.

"They open and close with the sun." Feeling amazed by my own ignorance I threw my hands toward the sky. "How have I never noticed?"

It's truly extraordinary what you can walk by without noticing.

I'm heading out for a second go at the Appalachian Trail this spring. Since my last walk, I've become a naturalist by trade; guiding hikes in Glacier National Park and teaching kids about ecosystems at the Grizzly Wolf Discovery Center. These callings have opened my eyes to the wonder of the world that we live in. It feels powerful to be taking that with me on this next journey.

I look forward to noticing the healthy forests when I'm in them, and understanding what a big deal that is. I look forward to recognizing a bird call or two. The first time I hiked the Appalachian Trail I was in a hurry and spent most of my thoughts consumed by what I thought I had to prove. I laugh at those concepts now, knowing that a journey is a place to be. In every step.

I am guided by the great grey owl. I've known that for a long time. What I'm learning more and more from her is how to be stillness that moves. It starts with noticing.

Same, But Different

April 21, 2021

This is a bit surreal. I'm in Dahlonega, Georgia, reflecting on what's about to start tomorrow. Ten years ago, I hugged Jesse goodbye and left him my car, then flew to my cousin in Atlanta. Yesterday, I did the same, only I feel like there's no reason to look out the car window on the way to the trailhead and wonder about myself.

I know this road. It's a walking road of many steps. There will be strolling, eating, and confluences of people in their natural habitat. I'll have rocks, dirt, and water, as well as a brain telling itself stories. I hope for open ears to listen to the critters and eye contact with strangers across the table. We're here together, and it's now or never.

And so what? I'm walking from Georgia to Maine. I could be raising a toddler or traveling with a rock band. I could have never left New Zealand. It happens to be this. I'm honored to be here and touched to be well received. Ready to celebrate being alive.

Ten years ago, I couldn't sleep. I wrestled with imposter syndrome telling myself that thru-hiking wasn't mine. Today, I understand that it isn't. It's all of ours. Or, more honestly, it's none of ours. We're borrowing everything we've got.

I remember climbing out of my bunk bed around 10pm to type my expectations before I started the hike. This time, I'm going to take inventory of what's different.

- I am less excited to eat all the Pop-Tarts I want without gaining weight.
- I actually paid attention to how much my pack weighs (Base weight 12 pounds).
- I know that I have it in me to make it all the way to Maine. I also know that my people will still love me if I don't make it past Springer.
- I'm hiking in a dress. I like dresses, and if I'm going to wear the same thing for five months, I don't see why it shouldn't be something I like.
- I understand that the trail is for now, and now is what matters. Five months does not feel like a long time.
- I have come to understand that all guilt is self-inflicted, so it's not walking with me.
- I have time. If I move fast, it will be because it feels good.
- I'm here to travel, and plan to take side trips like Ashville and NYC.
- I'm going to play every guitar I come across.
- I look forward to learning about the forest from locals.
- I'm not here to prove anything. I'm here to celebrate everything.

Then there are a few things which are very much the same.
- I'm still supported by incredible friends and family
- I'm still grateful for my health and choices
- I still live and die for Harry Potter
- I still look at thru-hiking as mostly an opportunity for eating
- I'm still my mama's daughter

Sara-Tide is here to send me off tomorrow. My cousin, Jess, picked me up from the airport and will be meeting me out on the trail in a few days to hike together. We are being hosted by my friends' generous parents tonight in Dahlonega. In the spirit of spontaneity, I decided at dinner tonight that I'm going to add on the nine miles of the approach trail tomorrow and do it as a run. What the heck?

When I was a teenager, I had a mentorship with the owner of a restaurant I worked for. We were busy, and I was supposed to leave to go sing with my high school choir. I told him I could miss it and stay. He said sternly, "When life gives you opportunities, you grab them with your teeth. Get out of here and go sing."

I thanked him incessantly and asked if there was anything I could do before I ran out the door.

"Just one thing." He said, "Show me your teeth."

Up Up and Away

April 28, 2021

I noticed right away how different it feels. Walking past wide-eyed hikers, I stopped to talk to them. I wanted to share. 10 years ago, I was hopeful. Now I'm home.

I told several hikers that they *are* walking to Maine, that they *are* thru-hikers. Though I recognized their questioning eyes and need to add "hopefully" to the end of the declaration.

"Definitely," I said, "Of course you can. You will." Which doesn't mean I don't expect a derailer. It means that I believe in us. This time it feels like I'm flying. Like I'm some kind of critter who was made for this. I believe we all are. We are born to walk, and our hearts know it, as well as our feet.

My cousin, Jess, and I played a game of cat and mouse where she started 40 miles ahead of me. It took me five days to catch her, and a good effort on all five of them. I had one *keep-moving-or-die* day in which I had to laugh at myself for inviting the Appalachian Mountains to remind me that they can be cold, no matter what I'm used to. I saw a rattlesnake. Fled from a place where I heard ATVs in the middle of the night. Had a girls' night in Hiawassee with two amazing women. And declared Trevor, the first friend I made under the arch at the very start with his two dogs, to be my best buddy on the second day. The AT is already showing me many of its colors. I'm honored to be here.

And Then What Happened?

May 5, 2021

Love exists in surprising forms. Perhaps nature is the easiest one for me to access. It feels like all I have to do is breathe, or step. Yet, it turns out to be the thing on your mind, or the thing in your pocket, or the memories that walk with you. Then it picks you up on the side of the road or swells with joy when your voice comes through the tiny slots in your phone.

Yesterday, I was getting ready to walk back into the woods in a raging storm, on the south boundary of the Smokies. My plan was to move quickly in the rain and catch my cousin who was half a day ahead. If you know the area, you might have a bone to pick with that. These mountains contain unique beauty and deserve your time and attention.

I stood at a trail kiosk, pondering my choices.

I do like to move, and it often feels like a celebration of who I am. Still, a good cousin is worth their weight in gold; the built-in friendship, the context of a shared upbringing, the wiring that is genetically similar; all things you can't build. I had already felt a new calling to slow down while in Jess's company. That's why I came here, after all.

As I stood on the side of the trail in the pouring rain, I heard, "Hello," in a familiar voice behind me.

"Jess!" I squealed. I was equal parts concerned and thrilled. "I thought you were 20 miles from here. Are you okay?"

She was smiling and walking, so there was that much. I soon learned that she had spent a stormy night in the woods. Her sleeping pad had become a lifeboat as her tent filled with water. A tree limb landed close to her head, putting a hole in the rainfly. She spent hours of the night holding the walls of her tent out while the wind whipped violently. And now, through the tight hole in the hood of her rain jacket she smiled and asked if I wanted to hear a song she wrote about it.

We walked back across Fontana Dam with a gait of giddiness. I had to work hard on not peeing myself through the rampant laughs. We played our family game of shanghai last night and made a non-plan plan, which we will kick off today.

I'm getting exactly what I came here for.

Little Has Changed

May 12, 2021

Sara-Tide and I are up to the same shenanigans as always. When we met, not far from here, we became trail sisters and walked together until central Maine. The bond between us was automatic then. Ten years later, it still feels special, to have a friend who's crazy like me.

In her endeavors to join me with road support, I've enjoyed celebrating life and sharing a beer with her at Clingman's Dome (the highest point on the AT), then another the next day at Davenport Gap. And one more on top of Max Patch. We sat there and dreamed about where we want our lives to go, much the same way that we did when we last walked this trail.

I wish I could send a post card to my 10-year-ago self. I'd love to show her a picture of Sara-Tide and I on top of Max Patch, working on our secret handshake and planning a walk across Scotland. Still in love with adventure, still not sure where the next walk of life is going to take us.

We dearly miss the other member of our 2011 trail family, Stephen.

In Vermont I'll see him and meet his partner and dog. Meanwhile, he is doing me the great honor of growing a surrogate trail beard.

It's good to be family.

Dining with the Dead

May 14, 2021

Lunch. On a Sunday afternoon. I picked a spot next to two headstones. I thought that would be the right kind of company to process some thoughts.

They are a couple, I'm pretty sure. George and Eva Gragg. She died on November 3, 1940, but her headstone says *Absent, Not Dead*, which is why I knew I could talk to her.

I was troubled by my own intensity, or more so, how it's perceived. I have German blood, a convicted tone, and a desire to be alone. To camp alone and walk alone. It's not because of a negative response to togetherness. I believe in community. I know that we need each other. I love people.

Yesterday evening I came to a picnic table full of hikers dining in front of a shelter. It was 6pm. "Just in time for dinner" a familiar hiker on the corner of the bench said.

Dinner with friends is a lot of thru-hikers' favorite part of the day. There's generally good stories and you get to witness the ever-impressive variety of meal ideas that hungry walkers concoct.

I ate my Luna bar standing at the head of the table in solidarity and told them I was moving on. Then I got a ping of worry in my gut that choosing to be alone can land like rejection on listening ears.

I'm ready to carry less of that. I'm not responsible for how anyone else feels, and I've come too far not to be myself. I do have sharp edges and I don't want to hurt anyone with them, but I have soft ones, too. And I'm doing the best I can.

Just around the bend, after saying goodbye to that group of hikers, I found a woman on the ground. She was laying on her back with her shoes off and a smile on. One foot resting on her pack, she glanced back at me over her shoulder. Various hiking items were scattered about the steep angle below her.

Step one, I've learned, is the mantra of my idol teacher in emergency medicine. *Don't just do something, stand there.* I took a deep breath. "Are you okay?"

"I'm fine." Her vocal tone would have fit in standing in line at a grocery store. "Just waiting for the pain meds to kick in and then I'll walk on."

She told me the story of the ankle injury, well, me, and the man behind me, who came to her almost immediately after I did. I tested the sensory and motion in her injured ankle, he asked smart questions, and we both offered care. Actual care. Where we listen and comfort, and we ignore her refusal for help.

After moving her back on the trail and collecting her splayed items we practiced walking a bit. She could do it, but it hurt. It had only been 15 minutes since she swallowed four ibuprofen. She wanted to wait a bit longer before walking to camp and insisted that I leave her by herself.

Now, while dining with the dead (or absent, rather), I sense my own perceptions being under a microscope. There might be a hard-working jerk in me that's proud to be lonely, and maybe I run with her a bit excessively.

It's too easy to convince ourselves that we're undeserving of care. That woman insisted that she needed to walk herself out on her own. I gave in because I wasn't going to insist a fourth time, but still, the next day, I'm processing some gravity. If I could do it over, I would look her deep in the eyes and say, "You, as much as anyone in the entire universe, deserve support."

The Animal That I Am

May 15, 2021

The animal I am now is something else. My wild is wilder. My free is freer. My happy is all but offensive.

I feel strong and adapted. I feel ready, shaped for this. This turns out to be my life's work. I've been walking.

I'm not talking about my body, rather my tolerance. Cold is yes. Rain is yes. Mud is yes. What else is there? When I set out in the morning to walk certain miles, I set out with hope. Maybe that's the back side of doubt; heads hope, tails doubt. But I don't toss the coin anymore. I hold it up to my heart like a compass, heads up. That's my red Fred in the shed. That's the animal I'm committed to being.

Last Monday, I was having lunch with a friend in Hot Springs, North Carolina. Hikers across the patio said, "Hey Kiddo, is it true that you're going to be in Erwin by Wednesday? We're planning on doing that in a week."

"In theory." I laughed. "Yet, you may have noticed it's 1 pm and I'm still not walking toward Erwin." I looked in the direction of the French Broad River to comtemplate 69 miles by 4pm, the day after tomorrow. I nodded. "Yeah, I'll make it."

I was there by 1:30pm. The key is believing. I finally understand that.

It's not circumstances. It's not money, time, age, or gear. It's my brain. I always was the only thing in my way.

Tremendous

May 21, 2021

Sure, this endeavor is physical. That's the part we answer the most questions about. The mileage, the temperatures, the states, the stress injuries, the animal encounters- all measurable details which most hikers were already reciting on constant reel in their heads. I finally have the space and time to sit with my thoughts and I find words difficult. I hope to honor the immeasurable.

I was walking along minding my business, which happened to be hunger. It's here. I don't want to admit it, but I was thinking about junk food. The kind that really didn't appetize me at all a month ago. Cherry pie, to be precise. You know the ones that come in a little paper box, 390 calories, and typically acquired at gas station? "I could really go for one of those right about now," I said out loud then laughed at myself. "Welcome back, Kiddo."

I was on a hearty itinerary that day, 34 miles through the Roan Highlands. I knew my mileage was somewhere in the low teens and was approaching lunchtime, which meant over 20 miles to go. The biggest climb of the day was after the next road crossing.

I caught sight of the road. Debating whether I should hold out for lunch on top or stop to fuel up for the climb, I noticed a white van waiting at the bottom. It had an AT license plate and hiker friendly symbols on its side doors. I tried to cool my passions. As a vegan now, I do better if I accept that I'm un-feed-able (in life and on trail) and then if there happens to be something I can eat, it's a pleasant surprise.

A man popped his head out the driver window. "Got some trail magic for you." He made his way to the back doors and swung them open to reveal a hiker's lounge. A futon sat perpendicular to the back. On the floor near the boot was a cooler and a plastic bin full of snacks. And guess what was on top?

Cherry pie.

"I have plant-based jerky left over from trail days if you would like some. There are cold beverages, just give it a good pull to get it open."

I stood with my mouth hanging open for quite a while before I realized it. "Wow." came out weakly, "Thank you. I'm a vegan, actually."

"Well, there you go. Take as much as you want. And take a load off."

He patted the floor of the van. I obeyed then reached for an orange soda and the cherry pie.

The man was a trail legend named Robert Bird. Known for his generosity far and wide. He had a hostel in Massachusetts for years, called the Birdcage. Where he charged every hiker no dollars and declared that he feels moved to pay it forward and hopes we continue the gesture. He's also fostered six teenage boys in his lifetime. People like this give me more than hope, they give me peace and gratitude.

"When you get to The Station, ask if there are any hiker-donated rooms available." He smiled. He didn't treat me like I was crazy to think I would make it there that evening, even though we were 21 trail-miles from it. He was right, too. When I arrived at 8pm, after a glorious walk through some vast highlands that reminded me of certain tunes about certain hills being alive, some nice people I will never know the names of bought me my stay. I played the guitar and ate fries, thinking about humanity.

High mileage days were part of a mission to meet Bob Peoples. He has a bust in the AT Hall of Fame for his dedication to helping hikers. His efforts lead thousands of volunteers in hundreds of thousands of hours of trail maintenance. His hostel, Kincora, is tucked into the woods, all but swallowed by plants and animals. One of my biggest regrets of my rushed 2011 hike was not making time to make his acquaintance.

When I arrived at his vine-covered house, he greeted me with a smile. He charges five dollars, no matter which space you claim, including a tree house or separate apartment. He drives hikers down the switchback mountain road to the grocery store every evening and insists on doing your laundry. Above and beyond, right? And to top it off, Bob makes you laugh. He sits with you on his patio like you're as family to him as anyone ever was.

A man I was told to look out for as trail royalty was there at Bob's hostel, Nimblewill Nomad. At age 82, he is setting the record of oldest to thru-hike the Appalachian Trail. I'm not sure how much the record means to him, he simply keeps walking. He speaks with tears in his eyes about the blessed life he's lived and recalls funny moments with Bob over the decades. He's quick-witted and kind. I would list some of his hiking experiences, but it will hurt my wrists. He has more miles than anyone I've heard of.

There's so much love out here on the Appalachian Trail. I'm in Damascus, VA for my seventh zero day. Last time I hiked this trial, I took nine days off for the entire summer. It's been a month. I'm glad. Also, I've gained a pound, which feels like winning. But none of that matters. What matters is that we're all here, being together, while we've got the chance.

Holed-Up

June 9, 2021

Who do I want to be when a gift arrives? Do I pause, do I give it honor, do I tell it thank you? Or do I treat it like something I don't have time for? I have a choice to either behave like it's a roadblock or appreciate the twist in the path.

Last Friday, I strolled into Woods Hole Hostel. I had beautiful memories of this place and a bit of a woman-crush on the owner, Neville Harris. When she walked up to me with an asking grin the next morning, I felt the *yes* before I heard the question. "Would you be interested in a one-week work-for-stay?" she asked with her arms holding themselves across her chest. She saw my eyes light up, and I laughed about impulse, and how I should think about it before jumping. She said, "Wow, good job. Teach me to do that." And we agreed that I would walk on it. I hiked 13 miles that day and returned to Woods Hole.

I knew I was going to do it. A chance to pause and sink in was just right. I was starting to get a bit competitive with-well, I'd say myself, but honestly, with no one. I was falling into something false, imaginary. Miles, just because.

The day that I walked in, I abruptly stopped myself trail-side to write one paragraph. Catching myself in a dialogue that there's no time. "What the hell are you talking about?" I said to myself out loud. "Sit down! Write!" And then I wrote this: *There is a rushed separateness that I'm creating. I would like to make more effort to pause and feel and be.*

Then came a garden and a smile and beautiful souls that wanted me to stay. Thank you, Woods Hole. I've had tears and animal cuddles, laughter and fresh lettuce. There was music. I remembered the truth under it all. That this right here is the good stuff. I met over 100 hikers with time to see them. I didn't realize I had been poisoning myself with a thought pattern. On the trail, just days ago, I would try to avoid other hikers. To the extent of skipping a water source if there were people at it. As though spending time with them would knock me off my cloud and my connection to the earth was something to be protective of. Then I came out of the woods with sing-alongs in the shower house and gratitude circles before each meal. With gladness for the nourishment.

Neville taught me how to bake her grandmother's bread and encouraged her helpers to stay kind in the face of apathy. We felt like siblings, and cooked together singing along to Stevie Wonder tunes, dancing the magic dance of a crowded kitchen. A place where food turns into a currency of love that can be passed around. Which is the only real kind.

I'm so grateful for Woods Hole, and Neville, and the beautiful people I was family with for one grounding week of my life. There's a saying in the thru-hiking world: "If you want to go fast, go alone. If you want to go far, go together."

There is a Season

June 18, 2021

The heat is here. Fair enough. When it comes to spring in Appalachia, I've gotten off easier than the norm. For the first five weeks, I enjoyed cooler temperatures and bugless nights. Two weeks ago, the heat arrived and, naturally, the bugs followed. It's fascinating how Montanans melt in the heat. I went from rested and thriving to sleepless tossing and turning. Mostly it's the bug bites that keep me up, they seem to speak to me when I'm trying to sleep, but the warmth has contributed. I am a cold-weather creature. I would rather sleep in 40 degrees than 70.

Meanwhile, I know I would feel better if I stopped scratching. Which is a metaphor for my life. I give in to the itch, often times drawing blood. If I let it be, it would be over a lot sooner. I'm old enough to know better, but young enough to decide it's worth the bleeding.

Everything is part of it. One month ago, the trail was covered in may-apples, trillium, and magnolia pedals, now its blackberries, cow parsnip, and wild roses. There were cold rainy days, now there are warm, vibrant thunderstorms that follow the sweltering afternoon. I jump in every body of water that I can fit into. Even some that I don't, flipping myself from stomach to back, like some sort of hot cake on a griddle. I am eternally grateful that cool water runs down mountain sides. I'm also grateful that the Appalachian Trail allows a person to walk full days in the shade.

A lot of my hiking brothers and sisters have been asking me about quitting. They talk about having the Virginia Blues and ask what I did to get through it last time. I tell them that my friends and I mostly laughed through Virginia. It was the New York Blues that got me. I also tell them that I tricked myself in the mid-Atlantic. When I was focusing on how much I wanted it to be over, I was looking at gifts as though they were curses. I can remind myself of that, here and now.

Heat grows tomatoes. It hatches bugs, yes, and bugs pollinate plants. Plants feed us. Rain keeps us alive. Now that I've lived through the kind of wildfire seasons we've been seeing out west, I hope to never say anything bad about rain as long as my mouth makes words. Acceptance is the best adaptation nature ever gave me. I can whine about my itchy shins all I want, but then I'm just as small as the no-see-ums. Walking up hill doesn't hurt. Apathy hurts. Missing out on being alive hurts.

I know there is no way to fully appreciate privilege while you have it, but I want to try with all my might. My legs walk and my heart beats, and water falls from the sky. I have everything and I hope it shows that I am deeply grateful for it.

Thanks to the summer heat for kicking my ass. I look forward to the next couple months being a brat about it and hope to get smacked out of it as often as possible. Thanks to my friends and family who put up with me. May we welcome summer with itchy arms and blistered feet.

Host

June 27, 2021

Invite it all.

Invite the discomfort, the messy, even the icky.

Invite the exposed, the embarrassing, and the not-so-graceful.

Invite the miscalculation, the unrealistic, and the sass.

Invite the dramatic, the poor-form, and don't forget the hypocritical.

You might as well laugh. Do more than laugh. Enjoy it.

I'd say invite the ego, but it already invited itself. Rather, treat it nicely. Give it a seat at the party like anyone else.

Invite fear. Be kind to it. It never meant to hurt anything. It loves you a great deal. More than it can stand, sometimes.

Invite the ache. In fact, give the ache the comfiest chair. Keep its drink full and hang on its words. This is your guest of honor.

We owe this whole party to the ache.

It's the emptiness we fill. Where art is put on canvas. Where songs are born. The place where we are raw.

Invite the blood. It's full of life. Edgy. Inarguably real.

Be a good host. Invite it all.

Maybe courage will show up. I hear it loves a good party.

Maybe wisdom will recognize the opportunity.

Maybe peace will be drawn to the gathering.

Maybe.

May be.

Outside, the owl is watching. Content. Full of love.

Invite it all.

My Bottom Line

June 28, 2021

When I was in 10th grade, I had an exceptional English teacher named David Devine. He was the right combination of loving and harsh, bringing life messages that were what I needed at the time. "Think of the world" was one of them. "Only boring people get bored" was another. There was also a charming anecdote about his toddler working hard to produce the content of a full diaper, to illustrate to a high-school-brain that you may have put in a lot of effort, but the result may be shit. He knew how to get through to us.

There was a project with Julius Caesar, in which we were meant to make a bottom-line statement. A set of words strung together that can't be broken down any further. "Julius Caesar is a tragedy because _____." That may have been one of my first experiences with brutal reasoning. Strip down a layer, not there yet. Another, still not the bottom. Strip again. "Julius Caesar is a tragedy because of the death of the conspirators." *Too vague.* Try again. "Julius Caesar is a tragedy because of the death of Cassius and Brutus." I took a step back and looked at my work. Something was nagging me. *Let's be honest, Cassius kind of deserved it.* There it is, "Julius Caesar is a tragedy because of the death of Brutus." I stood tall. Mr. Devine gave me a paternal smile along with those coping tools, teaching me to weed through the information, and it was working.

Now, I ask myself, what is this about? "I am writing this book because _____" This past week, I've been walking with the question. What is my bottom line?

Yesterday I was walking with a trail friend, Bard. We were inspired, after 24 hours of being a trail family of four. Sara-Tide, Seeker, Bard, and I had been weaving together for a day. This is something I have not done on trail so far. I told Bard that I might do well to listen, rather than speak. I know the earth is calling me to say something, but who am I to say it? He got fiery and challenged the doubt that's holding me back.

"Who, then, is entitled to say it? Someone who's spent more time with nature than you?" He coaxed. "If the trees told you something, say it!"

It's time to strip away the bullshit. I came here to be a love activist. I'm acting out because I'm sick of this. We're a family. There is no them.

There is no someday. We are here. If we strip away every layer what's left is love. Love is the bottom. I'm sure of it and I'm not apologizing for it. It is the rock that I stand on and I am not backing down. I came here to love everybody and to tell the truth.

Last night, the four of us had our dinner together on a rock outcropping. We enjoyed the sunset and talked about the animals we all are. An owl, a bear, a dog, and a kitty. We wrote an improv song about it and knew it didn't have to rhyme or make sense. Then we closed out a beautiful day singing *This Little Light of Mine* in harmony. I felt alive in the deepest, truest way. I felt love for those three, love for myself, love for life. We were love. The four of us in the new darkness, letting our light shine to the Shenandoah Valley.

I believe we are coming together. I believe we are ready to rise.

F Words

July 5, 2021

Extremities. Yes, for it's been a scorcher. Mostly, however, I want to talk about old friends and new family. For the last week we've had a heat index in the 100s and dropped low in elevation since the Northern boundary of the Shenandoah ridge. I've developed a strategy for the mid-Atlantic. Keep your head down and hike. I'm in a hurry to get to higher ground. Yet, I'm already questioning that theory with the memories of my beautiful trail family for whom I am five-days-lonesome.

It's good to hike alone, and this is my first big chunk setting out without visitors. I camped alone each night and stopped when I felt like stopping. I thought rather than spoke. I appreciated the freedom of doing things my own way. Valuable ways to live, I suppose, but I find myself asking, *freedom from what?*

Sara-Tide offers the most powerful friendship, the likes of which I have rarely seen. Despite the boisterous life I've had and the incredible women that raised me. She is one of my favorite living people to walk with and I count myself deeply lucky for her company on this journey. It feels appropriate to have her in my family on this thru-hike.

She is now working as a ridge runner in the Shenandoah stretch. A guardian of the trail, looking after its maintenance and the way hikers treat it. Getting her perspective and meeting her people was insightful and straight-up luxurious. Ridge runners are a valued part of how this trail is so well-cared for.

Sara-Tide also happens to be an adventure saurus. We will continue to get after it together for years to come. I know no other woman more experienced with the great, wide out-there.

Bard, Seeker, and I aren't done walking together. I know that. In fact, we're meeting up in a few days to take a zero. I don't think I could have asked for two more thoughtful, kind men. The same themes are on our minds. As though we're taking the same master class in life and are forming a study group. We compare notes about relationships, family, spirituality, death, and what we're learning about ourselves. We don't hide or edit, we share.

It's good to be a family.

Empty Chairs

July 16, 2021

Though the trail has been good to me I've been heart sick for my family. This week I've walked through AT landmarks that held memories from 10 years ago. Places like the Mason-Dixon Line where Sara-Tide and I shook hands as a northern and southern woman, or a road crossing outside of Boiling Springs, Pennsylvania, where my incredible family picked me up with my hiking buddies to join us for a few days. I recalled vividly the tall grass in which I hurled my backpack and hiking poles to run into a hug when I saw my little sister, Mackenzie. I laughed out loud, walking this week, at the memories of introducing my hiking family to my first and deepest family.

I stopped in my tracks at sights of emptiness. Particularly the table that Stephen and Sara-Tide and I shared for the *Half-Gallon Challenge*, now vacated. And me, passing through with a bitter-sweet smile. I recalled the talk I had with Sara-Tide on the way into Duncannon last time, about how grateful I was for my family. A sort of double rainbow of longing to be with them on the second walk in.

Memories flooded my eyes as I stepped into the woods north of Duncannon. It was there that I experienced my only overnight camping trip with my mother and two younger siblings. I was missing them dearly. We've always been a tightknit team. I came upon the spot I remembered taking their photo and sat for a good think, picturing their smiles.

My family has been through a lot since then, therein lies the sadness. I couldn't stop thinking back to the togetherness and the simplicity we had. Before cancer and mental illness and a divided political era, the four of us stood with wonder in our eyes. That's not gone, I know, but for today, it's missed.

A few days later, Seeker and I were invited to Bard's mother's house in the city of brotherly love. I think I cried eight or nine times on our zero day, being touched by the love I was witnessing in that house and the music we filled it with. The three of us along with Bard's mother and stepfather, sang spirituals in rounds. Often with tears in our eyes as our harmonies came together.

We celebrated Shabbat with Bard's mother and stepfather, both of whom are Rabbis. His mother broke bread and blessed the meal. We went around the table expressing our gratitude. I shared the joy I was feeling for one of my best friends finishing chemotherapy that day. Our hosts cried with me as I spoke. Then Simcha (Bard's mother) got up from her chair to place her hands on Bard's head and bless him. A blessing for the children. I watched in awe. Inspired and deepened to see that a family could be so open in spirituality, grateful to be open myself at their table.

I have been walking alone this week, but something feels different. I feel like I'm here, on the ground. I've arrived, with some sadness and hopefully some healing, yes, but mostly I'm here with the heaps of love that got me this far.

Long May We Walk.

Real Danger

July 28, 2021

I spend a good amount of time on a soap box about actual danger. I think I get this tendency from two major platforms of my life: my love for walking alone and my love of predators. There's so much fear in our culture, and I find the marketing of it to be rather askew. Statistically you are more likely to get crushed by a vending machine than killed by a grizzly bear. Yet, people who don't live in grizzly country are frequently insisting that they know the dangers that I'm up against.

It's best to take that as a protective and caring concern, rather than misinformation. It bothers me how much the media loves a sexy story. It feels unrealistic when people mark me in their minds as some kind of badass. It feels a bit hurtful when they accuse me of being less than smart for walking alone. I know what's out there, from being out there.

The things that are actually dangerous are so much less glamorous. Like slipping on rocks. I came around the corner to a woman sitting on a rock pile with blood dripping between her eyes. She was smiling and another hiker was tending to her, but still a reminder that the edge is closer than you think. It's kind of her to take one for the team and share that message with us. I sat with her and cleaned up some of her wounds, checked her for a head injury, laughed with her about our lifestyle and after her wife came to get her, I walked on thinking about danger.

It would be wise to take my time on these rocks.

Then I came across one of the two critters on the Appalachian Trail that can actually end you. On a hot day near Palmerton, I reached a beauty of a water source and took off my pack beside it. This is gold, having a piped spring flowing from the mountain side in Pennsylvania. These ridges don't run with brooks and streams and moss-covered rocks, as many AT ridges do. They are low, dry, rocky places. Meanwhile, there are warm rocks in the sun below me, and there's shade next to the water source. That makes it an ideal place to stay a while. I began to unpack my overnight stuff, soaked from the night before, and spread it out on the rocks below me.

"Yard sale," I sang to humor myself as I lined up my sleeping bag, silk liner, and tent along the slope. Then I took a seat next to the spring. I got out my book and looked ahead at the statistics of my day. It could be 18 miles until the next water source, if I didn't want to go off trail a good amount. The next stretch was a superfund site, I'd been warned. Those were not the streams or berries one would do well to consume. Not high on my list of fun facts.

"Time to flip." I pushed myself up toward my gear. I picked up my tent and gave it a bit of a shake, making a familiar rustling noise with its cuben fiber floor, and then a shot of adrenaline slithered through my spinal cord. A copperhead snake crawled carefully around my sleeping bag liner. It was stunning, and beautiful as gold and tan patches spiraled around the royal blue cloth. She didn't look at all aggressive, but it was unnerving. I shuddered and made moves to back briskly away, promptly retrieving my splayed items with a quick prayer not to be reaching toward venomous fangs.

The entire next climb made me jumpy. I was walking up a pile of rocks in the sun and wanted to see every cranny before putting my foot down.

The other critter that counts the most out here is the blacklegged tick. The Lyme carrier. That doesn't get news coverage like bear attacks or trail murders, but each year 30,000 Americans contract Lyme Disease. I was diagnosed with it in 2011, after my first hike. It is a real and present danger.

Perhaps the most dangerous thing of all is the basket-full-of-crazy inside our heads. Things like time goals, attachment, and vanity. I don't have any photos of the snake I saw the other day, because I don't think like that.

Yesterday I was standing on the highest mountain around in a thunderstorm, and all I knew was that I needed to get down. The hiker behind me thought making a video was more of a priority. I disagree. The idea of showing off the danger we come close to is a tremendous threat to our safety. Being attached to being somewhere at the time you thought you would is one of the leading causes of search and rescue parties.

Adaptability is much of wilderness survival. Like many things in the woods the metaphors for life are poignant. We do our best when we work with what's there rather than forcing what we want or have become attached to.

Danger looks so different than the things we worry about. A stranger can be easily made into a villain by a ridiculous movie scene in your head, while a person you've been trusting with your most vulnerable pieces can turn out to be a wrecking ball. Your heart can say a quick prayer that mountain lions don't eat you while a mosquito is giving you malaria.

I give myself a shakedown for attachment and try to shed some of it like extra weight in my pack. I check myself for stories like I check for ticks. Sometimes I find them. I'm sure I miss some, too. This is how I have come to rely on myself in the woods. Trust your gut and check in often. That's the best I know how to do.

Eight Hours in Manhattan

August 6, 2021

From the window of a train this time, my 3rd time, I approached New York City. Coming slowly in from the Appalachian Trail gave it gravity and a dreamy glow. That one could step out of the woods onto a platform, pay 22 bucks, then emerge in Manhattan.

The empire state building made it undeniable from across the Hudson. The city that never sleeps. I dug up memories and accessed mental pathways set when I was a teenager, moving here to try a life in musical theater. Sixteen years later, it's still part of my muscle memory, like riding a bike, and I stepped around port authority making a bee line for an A train, uptown, before even realizing where I was going.

The humidity and smells of the subway haven't changed a bit. Nor has the sound of its metal wheels jugging against the seams along the screeching tracks, while people stand inches from it without looking up from their phone. I felt it more than I heard it, the rhythm thumping in my chest. This used to be every day. Now my every day is foot patter and trickling water.

Fresh air is always the same when you're breaking into it from a place without. The breeze on your face, the understanding without words. *This. Here I am, 72nd and Broadway.* My school. My neighborhood. Where 18-year-old me landed fresh off the boat from the Midwest with a dream and a suitcase. And a lump in her throat.

Standing there now, in my hiking dress, I carried an empty stomach, a watchful eye, and a coyote smile. Equal parts enticed and peaceful. I looked up at the Ansonia building and said thank you, with lungs that I know how to use and soles that use me. The study of being human has never left my blood. This is where I got my training.

I found a falafel next, and went directly to the John Lennon memorial, pausing for reflection in front of the Dakota building. Imagine indeed. Now and always. I sat in Strawberry Fields next to the circle, and listened to Beatles covers while watching the other onlookers like myself. There's something about a New Yorker. Not just the way they wear their hat or sip their tea, but the way they sit on a bench like it's their living room. Sort of reminds me of the way thru-hikers sit on logs.

I thought of how I felt as a teenager trying to make it in this city on my own. I imagined her sitting beside me. If I could get her shoulders out of her ears a bit? Maybe just by sitting next to her with peace in my heart. Recalling the things running through her brain about what she *had* to do or who she *had* to be. I could just shake my head, "Nah." I'd say, "We're good."

Maybe she'd sink into that bench a bit. Maybe she'd close her eyes and feel the music vibrate. She'd smile. She'd hum. She'd be one of those specks in the wind, like other New Yorkers. I love that kid for her hope and her drama. She did alright with what she had.

When I returned to the trail the next morning there was a group of thru-hikers sitting on the ground against their packs, right next to the road crossing. Their energy reminded me of the pigeons in Central Park.

We talked about the city. I told them that, in a big way, it felt like moving to New York was my first thru-hike. I access the same wild animal; briskly walking to my destination, surviving, dancing with the obstacles. The learning curve was similar in that it felt huge and impossible upon arrival, then a short time later, I looked up at myself to say, "Wow. I'm *this* now." A couple of them chuckled and seemed to know what I meant.

We adapt. Perhaps I lose sight of that sometimes being set in my ways. It's remarkable how normal can change.

They say if you can make it there you can make it anywhere. I'm not sure what counts as making it, but I'm grateful to have started with Manhattan.

Ay Mi Familia

August 14, 2021

With entering New England came some of the happiest times I've had so far. My mother picked me up from a nice woman's yard in Salisbury, CT and stuck with me for 8 days. From Connecticut to southern Vermont, the feeling of home met me at each road crossing.

Seeker joined us for lots of comfy hotel sleeps and charming New England towns. The grand finale was a zero day in a condo with my trail family from 10 years ago, Dumbledore's Army. For the first time in years, we were together again; eating ice cream (cashew in my case), making music, and fighting evil.

Sara-Tide and I fell in love with Stephen's fiancé, Molly, right away. We bombarded her with big sisterly questions. I knew I was going to love her by the sound of Stephen's voice several months back. I didn't know that she would out-nerd me Harry-Potter-style or be so poised and graceful. Stephen struck gold.

Hugging my mother goodbye always makes me sad, but after doing so the next morning, I had Sara-Tide's comfort. Followed by a hike with the whole gang. It didn't take long for the five of us to be playful kids, shin deep in mud.

It was fitting to hike that stretch with Stephen. We shared our last night together in the same wilderness in 2011, before he got off trail. I sat with him in these trees with grateful melancholy, understanding that a different walk was about to begin. I never imagined we'd be back like this.

Of all the precious moments in my life, one of the most touching was on parking lot gravel with Sara-Tide and Seeker that night. She lit a candle and laid out a spread, while we talked about music and dreams, naming the songs we would like played at our weddings. If we should be so lucky.

The next morning, we had a similar scene for breakfast and a heart-felt goodbye. Sara-Tide had visited me trail-side for the last time, as she was off to work at the 2021 US Open in NYC. We both cried. I relate to her wildness and often leave our encounters feeling understood. From our matching kitty shirts to our experienced feet, I feel lucky beyond measure for this friendship.

A few days later, Seeker and I got picked up in Woodstock, Vermont by Stephen. The next time we looked up we were peering through our legs in downward dog. Seeker and I had moments of disbelief while looking around at the beautiful hillside farm we were practicing on. To the confident yet soothing sound of Molly's voice. I pinched myself a few times, but it turned out it wasn't a dream.

For the next three days, we were absolutely spoiled by the happy couple: slackpacks, family meals, Mario Cart night, dog cuddles, music, pints of Ben and Jerry's, plant identifying endeavors, and chipmunks that eat out of your hands.

It's crazy. Ten years ago, when I agreed to hike with two bright and shiny thru-hikers in Tennessee, I never would have guessed the warmth that could come with it down the road. How we're still laughing, still stepping, and still believing in magic.

The White Mountains

August 21, 2021

I approached the tough part of this journey with the best send-off possible; a hike with Stephen and Banner up Smarts Mountain. The mountains were getting steeper and more technical. There was no denying the truth of what's coming. The White Mountains.

I had a hard time accepting their difficulty last time. I felt offended by the need to use my hands to hold on to rebar or make three points of contact down short pitches with a heavy pack. This time I could at least remind myself to laugh at it, rather than feel personally attacked. It's not personal, these are rugged ranges.

I made it to Moosilauke the next day, the proverbial gateway into the tough life. I saw only beauty. Much of this experience has been made easier by mental preparation.

It is hard, no doubt. It's hard on the level that even though I remembered it as strenuous, I still felt like it was harder than I anticipated. Some things are like that, like the cold in the mid-west or the mosquitos in the Boundary Water Canoe Area. No matter how bad you think it's going to be, it's worse.

I settled in for lower milage days and signed up for a couple of slack-packing opportunities. I also saw a chiropractor, which eased chronic hip pain that was plaguing me. Seeker and I separated to go different paces. On the night that I caught back up, we were on top of Webster Peak. In silence, we sat under the mystic moon sliver as it drifted toward the twilight glow on the horizon. The stars came out. With mountain silhouettes encircling us and a cool breeze on our faces. It felt like the opportunity of a lifetime.

The next day we ran wild through the presidential peaks, including the infamous Mount Washington. We stopped at three different huts to drink lemonade and coffee and eat soup. It extended our already rushed day, which is not the way I would advise a trek through these glorious places. From peak to peak we marveled quickly and by the 20th mile, descending the jagged rocks of Madison ridge, I wished we had planned things differently.

We were on a mission to get to his friends' house in North Conway that night. And once we landed in the comfortable seats of his car, I was glad. Well-fed and sharing a converted bus, we talked about our blessings.

I cherish that feeling, when you've experienced a day that looks like a dream behind your closing eyelids. It's nice to have a friend to share it with.

Misty Maine Morning

August 25, 2021

I'm here. Now. This time. I'm sorry about last time. Probably it's all the same to you, but to me it matters.

It matters that I smell you. That I have time to taste the blueberries and meet the locals. That I laugh and drink PBR with your wily ones and talk about your wily ones with your maternal ones.

I rejoice when the loons call. I throw my head back to hoot at the thunder. I can't stay dry, and I don't want to.

This grass is so green I don't think about what's on the other side. There is no other side. Not this time.

I miss Mamma and Sara-Tide in every parking lot, but they walk with me anyway.

I miss Lu, but her ashes are in my front pocket.

I miss Montana, but that makes me glad. My family, gladder.

It's bitter-sweet, but I hope to miss all kinds of things and to never miss a thing. The magic comes when you begin to understand that all of this is possible.

We're together when we're apart. Though they say no two things are ever truly touching. So, tonight, I drink to the space between. Turns out we're always going to be there. It feels like somewhere.

If love isn't walking with me, then somebody drugged me good.

Truth

August 30, 2021

I told them everything because they were four women with gray hair and strong bodies on a ridgeline in Maine. Drawn to them by impulse without knowing what it was until they asked me.

"How are you looking so bright for a north-bounder?"

"I'm so happy." I put my hand on my heart and took a breath. Words jumped out of me like a dog that wanted to play. I paused to make eye contact with each of them. "I hiked this 10 years ago."

All four women leaned in. "How does this feel the second time?" One of them asked.

"Amazing." I meant it earnestly. Of all the times I've used that word, this one felt the most important. All five of us knew it. They were watching me like the 11 o'clock number of a powerful musical.

"What is it about this time?" another asked.

"It's being 10 years older. I was rushed and unhappy; mad at the rain, grumpy about the mud, ticked at the rocks. I was taking it personally, like these obstacles were in my way, between me and what I wanted. Now I get it. Now, I just... (I took a deep breath as they waited patiently) surrender."

Like four mothers, they smiled at me with their eyes. With warmth and gladness. With yes.

What We Carry

August 31, 2021

A journey is alive in every moment. Each step. Katahdin was not a place to reach for, it is a place to be, among many. What matters to me is what's been here, alongside me. This hike has been a celebration of what I've got.

I love my body so much it makes me cry. A little of that's sadness, for how I used to treat it, but mostly, it's gratitude. I get to walk. That's my honor in this human experience.

I carry a heavy heart only because it's so big, and there's room for everyone in it. My legs are strong. They have no choice.

I carry faith that this is what's real and what will always be. Sunlight through the canopy and mud in our leg hair.

I carried an mp3 player the whole time and only started listening to it in the 100-mile wilderness. My last three nights camping, in the dark, up against my dinner tree, I sang along and laughed at myself.

I carried a letter from my Montana family. I asked them in January to write something magic on a piece of paper so I could keep it in my pocket. I finally read it on Katahdin. *Sing your song* was in the center and statements about the love in my heart filled the rest of the page. This family is mostly composed of children, and it's astounding how deeply seen I feel.

I carried a tacky, blue, screw-top container. Translucent, unceremonious, and precious. It holds ashes. This is my fifth time walking across a country, but the first without her voice. I miss her voice. It was especially loud.

I feel distinctly quiet.

It feeds a sort of loop. It's painful to think about these hardships, but then it wouldn't hurt so deeply if we weren't so alive. So, I circle back to noticing and I say, "Thank You."

Thank you, heart.

Thank you, feet.

Thank you, Appalachian Trail.

Afterword

Top 10 Reasons the AT is the BEST TRAIL EVER!
August 30, 2021

10. **Rain that is warm.** I don't get this luxury in the Rockies. When it rains, I think about safety. Out here, I am wearing a dress to twirl. I dance.
9. **White Blazes.** Are you kidding me? Someone has done the work to make it so that I need zero maps or navigational tools to walk from Georgia to Maine.
8. **Towns.** I never have to carry more than two-to-three days of food at a time.
7. **Culture.** The Appalachian Trail world is full of jokes and lingo. Songs and taglines. History and stories. Festivals and challenges.
6. **Variety.** When you glance back at your hiking season and realize you've come from Rhododendrons to Cedars, it's quite amazing. Furthermore, when you look back to the dialects and roadside locations of Tennessee and find yourself next to Dartmouth, or being told to "Scram" in a Boston accent, it seems hard to believe that this is all the same walk.
5. **Water.** It's everywhere and it's life-giving.
4. **Hostels.** There are hostels in every small town along the way and they are extremely thoughtful toward hikers and run by powerhouse humans who know and love the trail.
3. **Magic.** They say the trail provides, but you wouldn't believe it until you see it. I've heard stories of hikers breaking a trekking pole and then coming around the corner, deep in the woods, to find one fully intact sticking out of the ground like the Sword in the Stone. If you ask, you get what you need.
2. **Green Tunnel.** I cannot stress this one enough. It is a luxury beyond measure to be able to recreate outdoors in the summertime, from sun-up to sun-down, without thinking about protecting your skin. Thank you, trees.
1. **The People.** From the tears of Nimblewill Nomad, to the supporting hands of Robert Bird or AT Gracie, this is the gold.

Thousands of humans put forth energy, support, effort, protection and care to make this experience happen. There are individuals swinging pickaxes and hauling rocks so that you can take an easy step, which you won't notice when you do. There are beautiful folks waiting at road crossings so that they can cook you a meal and offer you a cold drink. There are advocates and builders and believers doing what they do so that humanity can have a nice place to walk. At times I've feared that America is giving way to hostility, but that simply can't be. Not if this is happening. The Appalachian Trail is here to show us people. Strip us down to our natural state, and you've got beings who want to share. We want to help. We want to be a family.

Gratitude

Every thank you begins with you, Mama. Every breath, if I'm being honest. For this project I express deep gratitude for your professional editing mixed with maternal excitement. In all walks of life, we walk together.

Thank you to my father. There's a child in me who is astonished and tickled to be dreaming up a lifestyle with my dad. Your support has elevated me beyond the mountain tops. I'm grateful to get my crazy from you.

To my sister, Megan, thank you. Your insights and attention to detail have shaped this book. Your timing was a gift, an uplift during times of saggy. It would have been a different book without your guidance.

To the Raszba family. You have sustained my living and filled my heart. Thank you. Watching you all grow is a revelation that dreams come alive. Distinct gratitude to its matriarch, Shasta, for proofreading my story, in this book and in life.

To the Authors of the Flathead. I couldn't have envisioned a brighter opportunity than writers helping writers. Many thanks to Kathy Dunehoff and the dozens of creative souls who shared their words. Who knew there were so many of us in the same beautiful territory? How marvelous for us to take each other's writing so seriously. And to laugh so loudly that other teachers close our classroom door.

To Chris Crecelius. Nary a fellow walking this globe can provide such intellect, artistry, and style. Factor in your paramount kindness and sense of adventure and there's nothing left to do but bow in gratitude. Thank you for the maps.

To the illuminating power of Light of the Moon, Inc. publishing company and its beautiful mother-daughter team, Alyssa and Olivia. It's been an honor to work with such a dynamic duo. Your support stabilized my roots while growing my branches. I am lucky to wear your label.

To Sara-Tide, my wildest friend. May our torches never burn out.

To Seeker Ray Mini, your ability to swoop in and save my life is uncanny. Thank you for your wisdom, your words, and your company. I'm grateful for the silent wings that brought us to friendship.

To the guardians of the trails; the Appalachian Trail Conservancy, The Pacific Crest Trail Association, the Continental Divide Trail Coalition,

New Zealand's Department of Conservation, and the Te Araroa Trust. Among those labels are countless clubs and teams of generous humans whose commitment to our precious lands has made the world more wonderful to walk in. May your silent heroism come back to your hearts in abundance.

To trail angels. We call you this when you hold out an offering of a sandwich or cold beverage on hot days. But I hope you've been continuously told how offering your kind eyes saves lives.

To stranger-friends. I've had the privilege of borrowing a bucket seat in your car and a bed in your home. To hear your story is a treasure; an opportunity to be a special kind of alive.

To those I've walked with. The words we shared were stamped into the ground with our footprints. May the beauty of our intentions be present in the soil. May many things grow. And may you always feel me walking with you.

To the Wilderness Act and those rascals Teddy and Gifford. I don't want to know what we'd be without you.

To Mateo. For shining his light in my direction. I am blessed by the heart you carry.

To the four directions. The Eagle. The Coyote. The Black Bear. The Buffalo. Wind. Fire. Water. Earth.

To my spirit guide, the Great Grey Owl. May my words be an offering to your silent wings and luminary vision.

About the Author

Shayla Paradeis believed she was going to be a Broadway actress from age three to 21 but found herself in a conservatory theater program in Manhattan daydreaming about fir trees and mountain streams. Shortly after graduating, she answered the steady drumming in her heart, not to Broadway, but to the wild. She moved to Glacier National Park, Montana.

Love for hiking trails soon became the current of her life stream. By age 34 she had hiked five long distance treks (the Appalachian Trail, Pacific Crest Trail, Continental Divide Trail, Te Araroa, and Haute Route) and hundreds of journeys through her favorite lands in Montana. She worked seasonal jobs as a hiking guide, nanny, and bartender in between thru-hikes every other summer. She is now blessed to call herself a naturalist and chronicles her adventures in the form of essays, poems, public speaking, songs, and a book or two.

Beyond any numbers on paper, she is committed to sharing her truth. She wants you to know that she's not a badass. Not even a little bit. She's afraid of heights, deep water, momentum, and exoskeletons. She cries often. And though she's walked all over the place, she hasn't earned her triple crown (term for a person who has hiked the AT, PCT, and CDT). She missed a section on the CDT in 2015 when she realized she was holding a goal over her head as though it could prove her worth. What's truly beautiful about Shayla is that she knows she's beautiful, even when she's binge eating chocolate chips. She wishes the same for everybody.

She has managed to make it all those miles without a smart phone, and to have lasting friendships and connections while refusing to send text messages. You can find some of her writing on the Sleep in the Dirt Blog by Big Agnes or in the We'Moon calendar. She is also a featured guest on Backpacker Radio through thetrek.co. You can visit her original blog posts through atkiddo.com. Her songs can be enjoyed on her You-Tube channel: Shayla Paradeis. Or you could go play outside. Whichever.

Signed copies of
Footprint of a Heart
available at atkiddo.com

www.ingramcontent.com/pod-product-compliance
Lightning Source LLC
Chambersburg PA
CBHW070710130626
46553CB00005B/1920